# HIGH FLYING ADVENTURE EVERY ISSUE!
## Rob Hanes Adventures

Included in *1000 Comic Books You Must Read* by Tony Isabella!



As a globetrotting private investigator for Justice International, Rob Hanes travels the world on assignment, facing adventure, intrigue and romance at every turn...

### ORDER YOUR SAMPLE ISSUE NOW!

Every issue self-contained—jump in with any issue!

Issues are 24-32 b&w pages with full color covers.

15 issues and 2 trade paperback collections published to date.

All back issues still available. Order all 15 issues for $39.99, or all 15 issues plus the trades for $49.99—totaling nearly 35 full-length stories and more than 450 pages!

To order, read samples, and learn more, visit **wcgcomics.com**.

"One of the industry's quietest treasures."
—R.C. Harvey, *Rants 'n Raves*

All art © 2015 by Randy Reynaldo

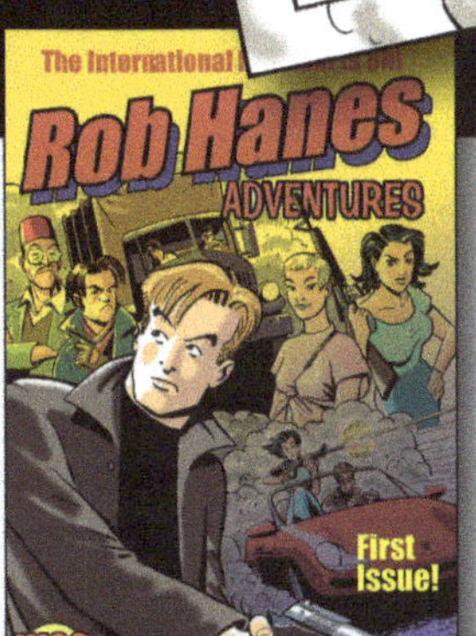


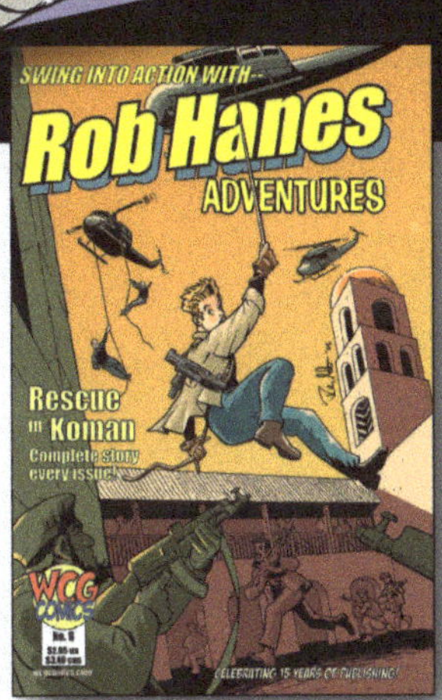

**Order a sample issue now at wcgcomics.com!**
WCG Comics • Dept. MLA • 10736 Jefferson Blvd, Suite 403 • Culver City, CA 90230 USA
Facebook: facebook.com/rhadventures • Twitter: @randywcgcomics

# TACHYON NODE

Tachyon Node is a 'Zine Publication. Not quite a Fanzine and not quite a Magazine, but a blend of both. It is a collection of short stories (all genres), artwork, and articles. It is meant to be a bridge, conduit, and gateway to all speculative fiction and thought-provoking ideas. Tachyon Node is a dimensional nexus of the multiverse.

## "Welcome to the Node"

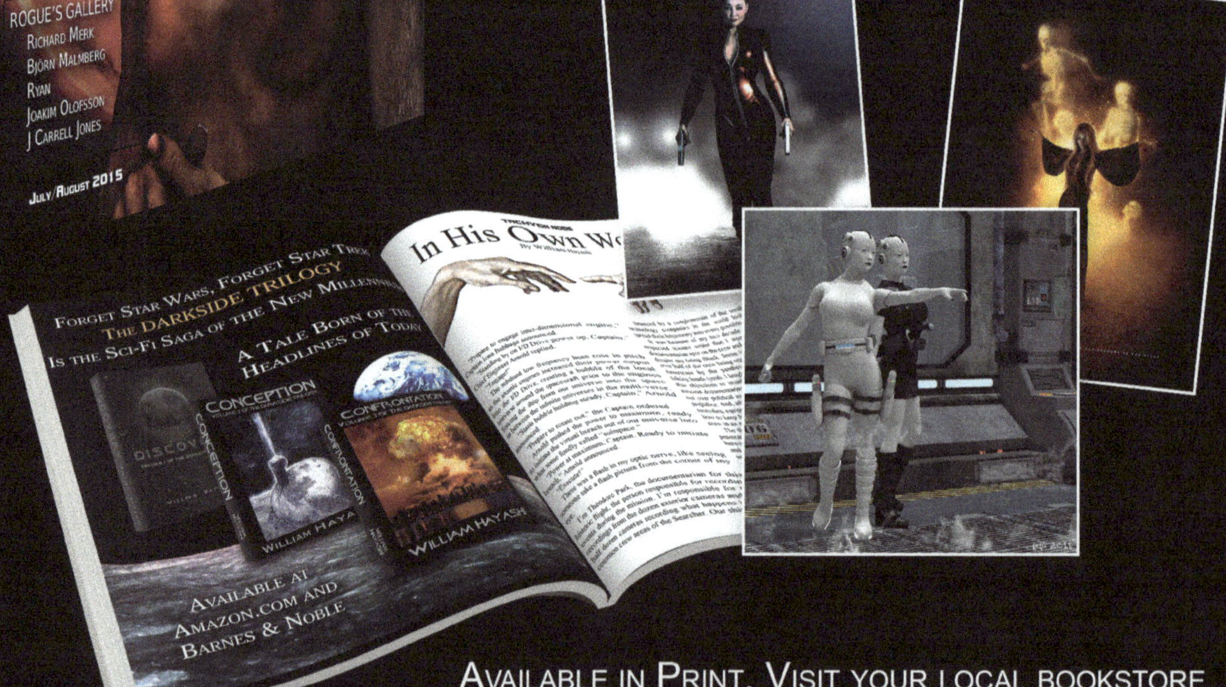



Available in Print. Visit your local bookstore or purchase direct from http://mythicallegends.com

# CONTENTS

**Tachyon Node Volume 1 Issue 2**

**December 2015**

ISSN 2379-982X

**Mythical Legends Publishing**
*First printed 2015*
P.O. Box 1667
Inglewood, Ca. 90308

J Carrell Jones, Publisher and Editor-in-Chief
Editorial Staff
Patricia I Williams, Reader
Kristy Victoria

**Contributing Writers**
Moshe Prigan
Patricia I Williams
Brandon Hill
Kenneth A. Strickland
J Carrell Jones

**Cover Art** by S.A.

**Contributing Artist to Rogue's Gallery and Content**
Björn Malmberg
Ryan
Richard Merk
Joakim Olofsson
J Carrell Jones
JPL/NASA

Article/Story Submissions:
Publisher@mythicallegends.com
**Advertisement:**
Ads@mythicallegends.com
**General Information:**
Info@mythicallegends.com or send snail mail to
Mythical Legends Publishing
c/o General Information
P.O. Box 1667
Inglewood, Ca. 90308

ISSN 2379-982X
ISBN-13: 978-1-943958-53-5

Copyright © 2015, published by Mythical Legends Publishing

All rights reserved. With the exception of excerpts for review or educational purposes, no part of this 'zine publication may be reproduced or transmitted in any form or by any means, electronic or mechanical, including photocopying, recording, or by any information storage and retrieval system. Please purchase only authorized electronic and hardcopy editions, and do not participate in or encourage electronic piracy of copyrighted material. Your support of the authors' rights is appreciated.

**Printed in the United States of America**

http://mythicallegends.com

## Dimensional Nexus



### PROJECT S.E.E.
(Space Exploration Explored)



### Rogue's Gallery



### Data Node



### Bibliography

Kelly King
Kenneth A. Strickland
Patricia I Williams
Brandon Hill
Moshe Prigan
J Carrell Jones

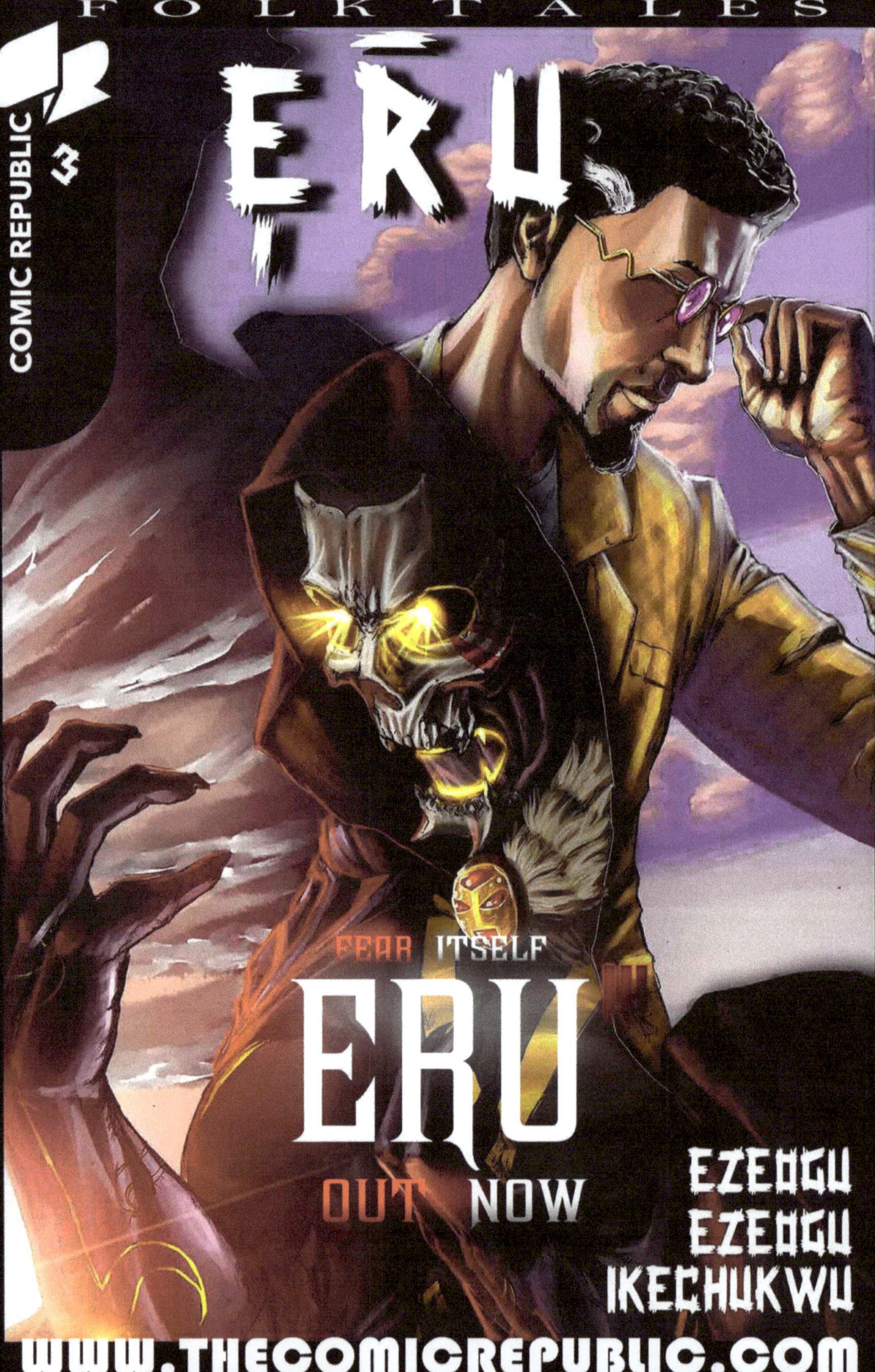
FOLKTALES
ERU
COMIC REPUBLIC
3
FEAR ITSELF
ERU
OUT NOW
EZEOGU
EZEOGU
IKECHUKWU
WWW.THECOMICREPUBLIC.COM

# Club Sensation

## Kenneth A. Strickland

### January 5, 1964

It was a rough year for Jimmy Holden. He'd spent it finding abandoned shopping carts, tying them together, and gathering bottles and cans to recycle. It took days of walking, and the last thing he wanted to do was spend it on anything stupid. He saw he had to do the work if he wanted anything.

He found old water hoses and patched them together. He found places he could hook them up,and used them to wash himself and clean the nearly worn out clothes.

He remembered what Bear told him. "Take care of yourself, Snake. Because when you stop caring, the world stops caring. Because right now, you are the world."

Jimmy took that to heart. He managed to keep going. He kept himself clean and frequented the library, reading everything. He might have been a freak in others' eyes, but he was going to take care of himself and not have to depend on anyone else.

He did find the shelter/help center Bear told him about. He made his way there and pulled his cart into the fenced yard that had a guard watching the other carts. Leaving the cart in a shaded area, he went inside. He never expected to see so many like him. They were all shapes and sizes. There were women too, something he never expected to see. Didn't know why since there were male mutants there had to be female mutants. It only made sense. There was a counter that was serving corn flakes and milk with thin pieces of bacon and toast and orange juice. They did require you to wash your hands, and Jimmy did so. He went and got the food, sat down and ate; even if the meal wouldn't fill him, at least it was food.

There was also the space where they helped you fill out the form for a state ID card. Yeah, over the last year he heard other mutants talk about how it didn't matter having ID since no one wanted to know who you were in the first place. But with an ID, he had at least an identity that was verified by the state. Say what you might, at least he would have an identity and could work from there.

Jimmy filled out the form and then stopped. They wanted a birth certificate. He didn't have one. He put his face to the table and thought, well that was that until he heard a sweet voice say, "Are you having trouble?"

Jimmy looked up and saw the smiling woman's face. She asked again, "Are you having trouble?"

Jimmy didn't know what to say at first. This was the first time in almost a year that anyone spoke to him. "Yeah they want a birth certificate. I don't have one."

She smiled. "My name is Mrs. Viola Davis. My husband's the Rev. Troy Davis. Made

this place so people like you can get help."

Jimmy couldn't stop the next question. "Why?"

Viola shrugged. "I guess that's the big question, isn't it?" She sat in the chair next to him. "We had a son that mutated. He and a lot of other people couldn't handle that. He was hunted down and killed by a mob that were led by people that thought he was going to hurt their children. But a mutant is someone's child. God doesn't like cowards. I guess my son didn't realize that I and his father weren't going to reject him. He still had a place and could make one of his own if he worked at it." She hugged him, the first hug he had in a while.

That hug shook Jimmy.

Viola continued. She nodded her blond head at the sight of Jimmy's shock. "You are only my enemy if I make you that way." She gave him a frank look. "You don't want any enemies do you?"

"No, I don't." Jimmy stammered still shaken.

"Good, neither do I." Viola said. "Now what we're going to do is get you your birth certificate copy. Meantime, I will help you get started with your social security card." She sighed. "You know, the world gets no better if we leave it as it is. If I can make a small difference in the ways things are where I am, then so much the better."

She smiled. "You will have to stay for a sermon, that much is required if you hang out here to eat. Trust me; there is none of the usual fire and brimstone act around here. We try to find what can make you a better person despite everything that happened to you. Anybody can preach about going to hell. But if we really want to go to heaven, we have to work on it here by serving the Lord, by serving each other."

"You really think that?" asked Jimmy.

"Do you really think that by screaming and carrying on that makes a difference? We start with gratitude, and then we continue by helping each other out. We can't do that if we are too busy treating each other like garbage. Now let's see how we can do this. First we get your birth certificate. That will take a few weeks because they have to go through the files. Now, we also have to work up the fees. It costs five dollars to get the copy of the certificate. Do you have the five?"

Jimmy stood up and dug into his pocket. He pulled several crumpled bills from his pocket. He had a ten and two fives and several ones. He handed a five over to Viola who had him sign the paper for the birth certificate.

"Now we have to get the social security card squared away." Viola said as she pulled another form to her that read "Application for Social Security Card". She handed it to him and marked the birth certificate form "Fee Paid" Jimmy filled the form and handed it back to Viola. She stacked it with the other form and took it over to the window where the clerk began to fill everything.

"Thank you," Jimmy said as Viola came back over.

"It's going to take time. Meanwhile, I suggest you start looking for work. In some cases, you might be a security guard somewhere or do janitorial work. I know it's not much, but it will be something. You might start your own business, and I think that might be your greatest chance. That way you don't have to worry about employment." Viola said.

Jimmy thought about it. She was right. He needed his own business. Right now, he wanted a beer.

_________________________________

The Club Sensation was a bar that was seeing decent days, it wasn't glamorous but still had a combo that played behind a well-endowed woman that shook her best assets to the music. The tall blonde was dancing to the music, and the sparse crowd was hooting and hollering,

Jimmy wore his best clothes and made his way to the bar and sat down where the light was low. This was one of those days the barkeeper didn't ask for ID and Jimmy ordered a beer. He nursed it while listening to the combo and ignoring the woman dancing, as hard as it was to do.

As Jimmy ordered a second beer, three men burst into the club waving guns and announced this was a holdup and pointed the gun at the barkeeper who tried to take a stand and was shot at. The woman behind the bar screamed and tried to call the police. One of the robbers moved to the combo and tried to take their money. The third went to the patrons, and demanded they give him what they had.

Then they got stupid. The robber on the stage hit the dancer and knocked her down.

"You stupid son of a bitch…." Jimmy snarled.

He sprung up and grabbed the robber that was trying to get money from the patrons, took the gun and bent it, and broke his arm. He then leapt for the robber with the gun pointed at the barkeeper and snarled, "You just had to come in here while I was having a bad day!"

He might be small, but Jimmy dislocated the man's arm out of its socket and growled at the robber on the stage. "I liked her dancing asshole!"

He leapt off the stage taking the third robber with him. The robber swung the gun around at Jimmy and got off two shots. One shot tore through Jimmy's shoulder and the second tore a gash on his scalp. Jimmy got the man's gun just as he shot twice more and tore it away. The robber tried to knock Jimmy down with a haphazard swing that missed. Jimmy caught the arm and twisted it behind the robber's back and slammed him to the ground. Baring his teeth, showing his fangs, he growled, "Don't do that again!"

Jimmy took the gun and tied it around the robber's arms then left him on the floor. He went back to his unfinished beer while the patrons applauded. Jimmy raised his glass to the small crowd and drank. He was putting on his hat and was about to leave when the barkeeper's Irish brogue asked, "Who do I thank for saving my bar?"

Jimmy knew it was too late to hide since they all saw what he looked like. "Jimmy the Snake."

"Saints preserve me!" the barkeeper said. "Never thought I'd owe a snake!"

"I just wanted a beer." Jimmy put the glass down. "That's all."

He was about to leave until the barkeeper said, "You look like you live in the street Jimmy boy."

"So far, I do. I'm at a shelter right now. I go out and hustle bottles and turn them in." Jimmy said as the others in the bar watched him. Jimmy wanted out now. 'Right now I'm waiting on my Social Security card and ID and my birth certificate."

"All of that? Aren't your parents helping you with that?"

"My parents threw me out."

The barkeeper stared for a minute. Looking as he did, it made sense that his parents would throw him out. They wouldn't want a son that looked as he did. "I can't do nothing about what they did, but I can offer you a job."

Jimmy stared and didn't want to believe what he was hearing. "My name is Mack Moran. I own the place and the attached hotel."

He looked at the robbers trying to sit up. "I need a good security guard around here. I figure you in a black suit and tie might just discourage troublemakers."

"A guard snake?" asked Jimmy.

"Works for me," Mack said. "You can even have one of the rooms in the building. You can even have Mondays or Tuesdays off. What do you say?"

"That can work," Jimmy said after he made a show of thinking about it. It was the best offer he was ever going to get in a long time.

"Mind you," Mack said, "In a way, when you're in the building you'll be on duty 24 hours a day. I'm looking to you to help keep trouble out of here."

Jimmy nodded. This was the best deal he's ever get, and he still could get his stuff here. The ID, Social Security and Birth certificate could still get to the help center, and he could bring it all here.

"I'll take it," Jimmy said. He held out a scaled hand to Mack, and the young woman he saw when he came in came over to them.

As he shook hands with Jimmy, Mack told her, "This is Jimmy the Snake, Maureen. He'll be our new body guard. Measure him so he can have some decent suits to wear on duty. He'll be staying in the hotel upstairs."

"Somebody to watch the place." Maureen Moran said. "Well we've needed that for some time."

She looked him up and down. "A snake huh? I wonder what St. Patrick would say about that?"

"Ah you're such a funny child! Take him upstairs and show him the room he can stay in. Measure him up for some suits, inexpensive of course. Oh yeah, and several pairs of dark glasses, that'll help with anyone looking to make a fool of themselves."

Maureen looked a second time at Jimmy's eyes. They were unsettling at the least, snake like but still blue yet with a yellow circle around the pupils.

Upstairs, Maureen had him strip down to his ragged underwear. She figured he needed underwear as well. She measured him from top to toe and assumed he needed soap to clean up. Jimmy made sure she knew he had to go and get his cart from the help center. Besides, he wanted to tell Viola what happened and of his good fortune.

"I'll get you a sport coat and some slacks you can wear tonight. Might as well get started. Be back here by five."

Jimmy gave a big smile and told her he would be back. He ran to the help center and told Viola what happened. Viola hugged him and congratulated him. Jimmy knew he would help out as much as possible. Coming here gave him a boost when he needed it. He owed that much. He went out back, pulled the cart to the bar and hid it in the back of the hotel, hoping no one would take it. He dashed back front where he met Maureen who had the sport coat and slacks. She led him back to the room and presented him with his key. He went inside, cleaned up and made his way down to the club. Mack showed him exactly what he wanted and Jimmy began his first night.

Jimmy proved to be a good guard. He kept careful watch on the goings on in the club. For some people it was unsettling to have a five foot upright walking talking lizard come up to you and let you know you were getting out of hand, for some people it was shocking to see Jimmy simply introduce himself as Snake and make his way through the crowd. Even teenagers who didn't want trouble realized the Snake was on duty and settled down. The ones that didn't round out the Snake took no prisoners. Just about everyone agreed he was a stand up man.

Jimmy didn't spend money much. Those ladies that wanted to "persuade" him to go a little easier on them, and they would reward him with their favors. He had little or no interest in women, and those who realized he wasn't after them, tended to be a little more respectful of him. Even the locals that came to drink tended to be circumspect when Jimmy was on duty.

Jimmy let those that helped him get help. Bear even began to come by, taking showers and getting in some sleep. After talking to Mack, Bear even learned to barkeep so that Mack could take a day off. The crowds were growing as the word went out about the two unusual men working at the Club Sensation. It was typical to hear "Big Bear!" when a regular came into the club. Sometimes all it took was a look from Bear at the bar to stop potential trouble.

Bear even came up with his own cocktail, a randy mix that set Mack back on his heels once he tasted it. They simply called it "The Bear" once Mack let him put the drink on sale.

The local mobsters started hanging out there because they knew nothing was going to happen.

Mack and Maureen were happy that the place was getting a reputation as a neutral space just to hang and be. Jimmy and Bear made sure of it. In fact it was not unusual to see Jimmy sidle up to someone and say, "I wouldn't do that if I were you." in the offender's ear. They would turn around and see the human-lizard face as it spoke and give them a grin that told them they didn't need the trouble.

In his time at the club, Jimmy grew three inches but he was still short. He took to wearing spats on his bare feet, along with polishing his nails on hands and feet. It helped give him a wicked elegant look that told people they were not to look for trouble in the Club Sensation. All in all, Jimmy and Bear did all they could to make the Sensation a place to go.

---

There was one night that did stand out in their minds.

Two of the local mobster regulars, Carl Maroni and Spence Draco came in the club with their boys. Bear gave Jimmy the high sign they were here. They knew they were relatively safe here.

"Big Bear!" Draco said as he came in and pointed a finger at him on his way to his seat. His table was on the opposite side of Maroni. Their boys sat at tables so they could have a greater field of fire as they watched their bosses.

Another came in as well. He was tall and slender with slicked back black hair and albino skin wearing glasses. He ordered a water with lemon and sat between the two tables facing the stage as a girl named Miss Skyliner did her thing.

Even Jimmy could feel it. The club was full tonight and the regulars were having a good time until Miss Skyliner finished and was making her way off the stage. That's when the albino man stood pulling a gun. Jimmy saw it and leapt as the gun man fired. Jimmy was hit twice as he managed to knock the gun out of the assassin's hand. The assassin's glasses fell off. The patrons stopped cold as they saw his eye; they were blood red and he turned and ran out of the club.

Jimmy hit the ground gasping. One each of the mob guard ran after the would-be assassin while the others guarded the bosses.

"The snake just saved your life boss!" one of the guards said as Mack ran over to Jimmy and tried to stop the bleeding.

As Bear ran from behind the bar and brought cold water, he poured it into the wound as Mack tried to pack it and stop the bleeding.

"I know that guy, boss, he's called the Red Eyed

Ghost, hit man for hire," another mobster said.

"Screw him, how is the Snake doing?" Maroni said.

"Not so good, he's going to bleed to death here if I can't stop this!" Mack said with tears in his eyes.

"Might I help?" asked an old voice. Mack turned to see a man in a ragged patched trench coat. He was leaning on what looked to be a long tree limb for support. It was shiny with wear and age. Sparse strands of graying hair hung limp from beneath a frayed knit beanie that may have once been white. The old man came from his table and stood over the bleeding Jimmy.

"Who the hell are you?" asked Draco as the old man dropped to a knee and took Jimmy's hand.

"Someone that can help this brave young one." the old man said as he held Jimmy's hand and closed his eyes. When he opened them they were white and the club could feel his power.

Bear could feel it and he didn't want to say anything. He knew what the old man was doing since he'd seen it before, once. Bear barely breathed as the power flowed and grasped Jimmy's hand tighter. His back arched and he lifted off the floor as a golden glow surrounded Jimmy. Bear knew he was witnessing one of the rarest mutants around, a healer.

The blood on Jimmy's body stopped and dried. The crowd could see the bullets work their way out of the body and Bear gathered them in a towel and pulled it away. He went and found a shot glass and dropped them in and held onto them for safekeeping.

Jimmy coughed hard and bent over double before he settled. The old man let go and stepped back.

"Stephanie, water." he said as he sat back on his heels. Someone was taking pictures with their camera as the old man finished.

"Master John, are you okay?" asked Stephanie as she handed him the cold water Bear drew for her.

"Is our young hero okay is the question." John said.

Jimmy looked at John with astonishment. "Thank you.

Master John smiled. "A brave one like you should not die so early in this life. I only honor your effort

at stopping the would-be assassin. Can you get up?"

Bear helped Jimmy to his shaky feet. Bear took him to a vacated chair and wiped his face as Master John smiled at Stephanie. "I think we're done for the evening."

Master John stood and followed the girl Stephanie out.

The two mobsters looked at each other and knew they owed Jimmy big time. They owed Mack as well since their assassinations were to happen in his club.

Mack said to the assembled, "All right folks, the show is over!"

He knew he would have to make a police report like it or not. After all the witnesses were spoken to and statements taken, the news was there and some of the reporters didn't want to believe what the witnesses had to say. Still this was big news if there were people that do what was described. But for now, they would settle for Jimmy and Bear.

Mack closed the bar. The two mutants looked at each other and knew they would be back in the morning to clean up. Mack told them to get some sleep.

As they trudged up the stairs, Jimmy looked at Bear. "You regret any of this?"

Bear grinned. "No. Life's been better with you Jimmy than without you."

"Good night, Bear."

"Good night Snake."

###

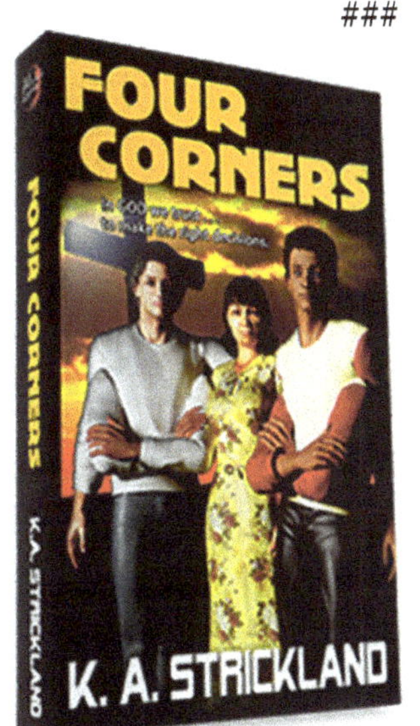


Available online, at your local book store or buy direct from us and receive a discount.

http://mythicallegends.com

Destined to keep alliances by marriage . . .
. . . then tragedy struck . . .
and a princess becomes a warrior.

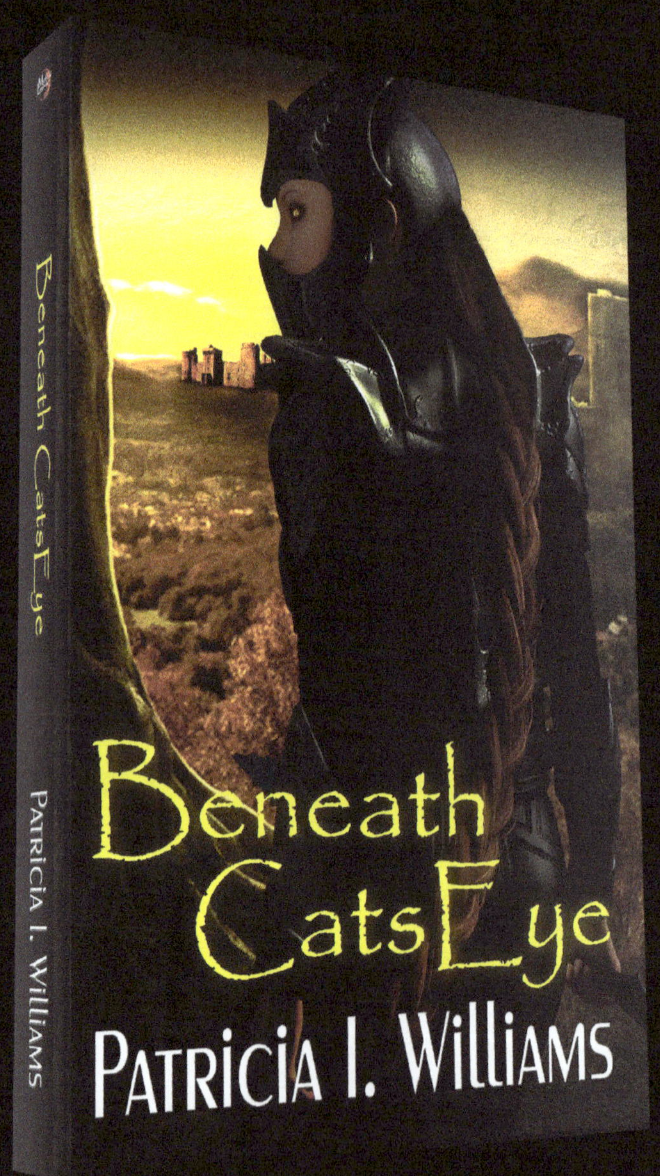


Available Online and at your local
Barnes and Noble Book Store

ariel-x.deviantart.com

THE RIVETING SEQUEL TO
"FROM SLATE TO CRIMSON"

DOUBLE-CROSS MY HEART

BRANDON HILL

A MISSION OF MERCY
FOR THE ENEMY OF HER
ENEMY BECOMES A
STRUGGLE FOR SURVIVAL.

AVAILABLE ONLINE AND
AT YOUR
LOCAL BOOKSTORE

# I Know Something You Don't Know

## Moshe Prigan

He met her at an exhibition of paintings in the local museum. She spent a lot of time looking at a small particular picture.

"I painted it," he commented noticing her interest, and then he apologized for distracting her.

"This one is awesome," she said, pointing at a small charcoal sketch of two girls sitting back to back on a dune among tall grass. Below was scribbled I Know Something You Don't Know.

"I'm flattered that you think that. Thank you."

"My name is Briana Cole. I teach art in high school," she said, offering a handshake.

"Dave. Dave Bonham," he said. She had a delicate palm with elegant fingers that he wanted the handshake to linger longer.

"Cup of coffee?"

Her smiling face acknowledged him. They went downstairs to the restaurant and he ordered black coffee while she asked for ice cream. When she gathered her silky long hair into a high bun he said he would like to paint her and she laughed.

"Do you paint?" Dave asked.

"I'm so exhausted after school that I just have no energy to do something, the more so to paint. I prefer going to exhibitions.

"This exhibition is my first public appearance since I lost my wife. I paint to overcome my grief."

"I'm sorry to hear that," she said.

"My wife got killed in a train accident a year ago, leaving me with my little 6-year old girl." He pulled a small picture out of his brown wallet.

"That's my little treasure, Maggie."

They chatted the whole evening and Dave learned that she was single.

"My ex-boyfriend tried to paint me but, the painting didn't even resemble me in the slightest way. I wasn't black and comely enough," Briana laughed.

It was the first time he felt some envy at the thought she had a boyfriend.

"How long have you been dating your boyfriend?"

"We've been together four years." Briana noticed he became restless.

"Didn't you think of marrying this guy?" Dave asked.

"I didn't want to get married, not then, and not to him. We just wanted to hang around."

"What were you doing the day you met him?" Dave asked.

"He actually met me, but why do you ask me that? I feel some jealousy in your tone." She leaned toward him. He liked the scent of her hair. She had milk chocolate skin and big shining eyes. Dave enjoyed looking at her.

"Maybe. See it as a compliment."

"I think you're …"

"Falling in love," Dave cut her off. Briana burst into laughter and then touched his wrist.

"Do you remember the earliest moment of your life, Bri? I hope you don't mind me calling you Bri," Dave said.

"I don't. My earliest …? What kind of question is it, Dave?"

"Try it."

"Who can remember" she said, waving her hand aside. She straightened her blouse over her pert little breasts.

"I don't want to sound conceited but I can. There's something seared deep in my mind."

"What is it?"

"I remember kissing you."

There was a look of surprise on her face at that moment.

"Are you hinting that we met up somewhere before?" she frowned.

"Yes, I am, we did."

"I don't think so and I don't remember that. Nothing comes to my mind right now."

"I do. I first kissed you when you were a baby, two years old. I was six. It was at the Baby's Health Center."

Dave leaned back in his seat, tapping his fingers on the polished table.

"No one would be able to remember himself at such an early age. You're just imagining that," Briana said.

"I'm not, but I can't prove it."

"You're so funny, Dave. I like guys who surprise me with some mystery."

Dave signaled at the waiter for another cup of coffee.

"And what would you remember from us meeting today?" she teased him.

"I think I already declared it, didn't I?" Briana smiled.

"You're lucky to have such a memory. I wish I had one like yours," Briana said. "I tend to forget things."

"I mostly tend to remember bad things."

"But you just told me you were falling in love with me. Isn't it a good thing to take away?" Briana winked.

"I wish I would remember. I do want to."

"You dare not," she said, hanging her head aside.

"And what's your earliest bad memory that you'd like to forget?" Briana asked.

"Me sitting in a stroller, aged four, pushed by my older brother. He bumped it into a wall and I hit my head."

"You have quite amazing memory."

"And I thought you would say you were sorry I had bumped my head," Dave laughed, pushing Briana slightly. She pushed him back. Then they embraced.

"I had an extraordinary memory in school," Dave said. "I could recite the Song of the Sea and Song of Deborah, but one summer day I forgot my daughter's name."

"How that happened?" Briana asked.

"We were at the beach and I called her Nicky instead of Maggie. I called twice but she didn't answer. Sitting close to me, a fat red-faced woman said: 'Why doesn't she answer you?' I felt confused."

"You painted a little girl encircled by broken letters, forming, as I now understand, her false name."

"Exactly. You have a good eye, Bri."

"And the painting with children and their decapitated parents, all sitting erect as if posing for a photographer …"

"You mean the one called Broken?" Dave interrupted her.

"Yes."

"What about it?"

"I felt uneasy. That's a horrific painting."

"I painted my worst memory, Bri."

"What is it, if I may ask?"

"I remember the day your mother was killed."

"What?" Briana almost screamed. She shoved her chair backwards.

"I was four years old when she got killed. We lived not far from your parents' house. You were the only black family."

"So we grew up in the same neighborhood," Briana said. "But why don't I recognize your face? Did you graduate Bridgeport high school?"

"I didn't. My mother couldn't afford that."

"Why not?"

"She had to stay home to take care of her three children, me and my brother and sister on one income alone."

"Where was your father?"

"My father was executed."

"Oh My God!"

"I saw him during his last moments. I remember me sitting on my mother's knees, crying. He was the first white male executed in Idaho."

Briana approached her chair and took his face between her hands.

"Why? What did he do?"

"Homicide."

"Jeese. I'm so sorry for you, Dave, and for your poor mom. Does she still live there, in Bridgeport?"

"We lived there until the homicide case of your mother. Then we had to move on."

"What did it have to do with my mother?"

"I'm sorry Briana, but my father murdered your mother."

Dave, noticing she was losing color, pulled out several wet tissues from the tissue box holder on the table and wiped her face, gently, slowly, as a sculptor making the last corrections of his work. He ordered a bottle of cold water and held it to her lips. She took small sips. She was slouched way down in her seat.

"We're two lost souls bumping into each other on one cold evening in a gallery," Dave said.

The restaurant workers started putting chairs onto the tables. Some of the last people just left.

"I have got to go. A long day is waiting for me tomorrow," Briana said. "I am going to take my class on a trip to the beach."

"I'll call and tell the school principal you fell ill."

"You're so kind, Dave.

"Would you wear a bikini?"

"With all the pupils around? No way." Now she fully smiled.

"Then I'll see you after tomorrow. We'll go for a swim, only us." Dave said. "We'll meet on the dock at five."

The humid night swallowed them up.

*

When Dave drove down the highway leading to the beach to meet Briana on the dock, he figured he would just have to wait about fifteen minutes for her. The beach was empty and the sun was already low. He had been waiting on the dock for her until the sun kissed the sea.

He drove to the gallery. She wasn't there.

After a week without a word or call from her, Dave decided to drive downtown and cruise the streets, to places where school teenagers hang out and shop. He entered the city mall and saw two young girls looking through the window at the clothes in a fashion store. They were talking loudly about buying new garments. Dave turned to them.

"Excuse me, young ladies; do you know a teacher named Miss Briana Cole? She teaches art."

"Sure, she's our teacher," squeaked the blond one, moving aside her tousled hair.

"She fell sick and has been taken to Saint Paul Hospital," the other girl said.

Dave sped through the maze of streets, ignoring several red lights at pedestrian crossings. In the reception, he was told that Briana Cole was resting at Ward B, Room 5.

He found her asleep, looking sedated. She was lying in a small room, with a window facing the Bridgeport dock where they were supposed to have met. He pushed a loose strand of hair away from her face and touched gently her cheek. Bri opened her eyes. As she saw him, she started weeping. Dave tried to soothe her, saying when he realized she hadn't shown up at the dock he figured something had happened.

She signaled to him with her finger. He put his ear to her mouth.

"I found my dead mother," she whispered and pointed at the bedside cabinet. Dave straightened himself up. The headlines on the front page of Bridgeport Evening Star read: "Human bones found on Beach Dowson." He fully opened the folded paper.

"Two school girls, being on a school trip to the area, found human bones in a dune. They were later identified as belonging to Miss Rose Cole who was murdered two decades ago and whose body has never been found. The killer, John Bonham, confessed to killing her but refused to reveal where he buried her body. He was charged on strong circumstantial evidence and was executed by lethal injection shortly after trial."

Dave took a deep breath.

"Remember my small sketch in the gallery with the two girls sitting on a dune?" Dave whispered in Briana's ear. She nodded.

"I painted the place where your mother's body was found. I titled it I Know Something You Don't Know." She slanted a look at him.

"Did you know something about my lost mother?" she asked in a low voice.

"No," Dave shrugged.

"It took about twenty years to find her, and she was found one day after we met."

"Strange things happen, Bri."

"You've been painting the sad stories of our families. You touched our lives with the same brush."

"They've come to an end, eventually," Dave said.

"Things got solved since we met," Briana said.

"Then it was a good thing we met."

Her smiling face acknowledged him.

###

FORGET STAR WARS, FORGET STAR TREK
THE DARKSIDE TRILOGY
IS THE SCI-FI SAGA OF THE NEW MILLENNIUM

A TALE BORN OF THE
HEADLINES OF TODAY

AVAILABLE AT
AMAZON.COM AND
BARNES & NOBLE

bovistock.deviantart.com

klil 2015

One Earth
Billions of humans
One human dies
We survive

# The Carhayaken Ring
# PROJECT
## Perpetuity of Humans

# PROJECT S.E.E.
## SPACE EXPLORATION EXPLORED
## The Carhayaken Ring
By Tachyon Node Staff

## Introduction

**The Ring should** be of significant size as to house a large and diversified work force. Its position in space will determine its usefulness in providing a platform for a variety of missions: Interstellar launches, deep system exploration, Asteroid mining expeditions, and exoplanet searches. The ring's thickness is measured in kilometers with a shell of metal, dense earth, and rock.

## Abstract

**The Carhayaken Ring** is a theoretical torus structure made mostly of earth and metal. The disciplines most likely to contribute heavily to its design, development, and construction would be physics, mechanical engineering, nuclear and photovoltaic systems, agriculture, Urban Construction, LEED, 3D printing and environmental sciences. For this paper the ring has a diameter of 10 kilometers and its intended purpose is to provide 1) Data for creating an eventual larger Carhayaken Ring, 2) an alternative option to sending humans to other planets, 3) provide extraordinary real estate for humans to use, and 4) an additional means to the perpetuity of the human species. The Carhayaken ring may be placed anywhere in the Solar System and within any orbit around any planet. It may also be placed in its own orbit around the Sun.

Currently, Earth is using up its natural resources at an alarming rate. Population has passed the 7 billion mark and current means of addressing food and water shortages are inadequate.

The idea of creating extraterrestrial real estate that would greatly and potentially enhance the quality of life for humans is intriguing. Population crowding would be the ring's immediate problem to solve. The access to an abundance of solar materials would solve resource scarcity for the ring and the planet Earth.

Creating a Carhayaken ring presents a multiple set of problems. First and quite obviously is that a construction project of this size has never been done on the planet Earth. The ring's construction and completion would have to be an International effort. Secondly, Earth would have to take an aggressive approach in completing the project. Even though current technology may be used in constructing the ring, said technology would have to be adapted to space travel. Also, some common mining techniques can be used be may have to be tweaked to work in a space environment. Mining and building is something humans have done for hundreds of years. Robotics would be heavily relied upon, but there would still be a need to put humans into space. Constructing an entire ecological, self-sustaining object of celestial size is something humans have never done.

For the Ring to be successfully completed, humans would have to cooperate at a level never before reached. The International Space Station was a test. The Carhayaken Ring would be of humankind epic proportion. Though several nations and International agencies would be able to start, construct, and complete the project, it would be of the upmost importance that all nations contribute to the construction of the Ring. There has to be International buy in either financial, materially, technologically, and/or with personnel.

## System Model

**The Carhayaken Ring** is a ring torus with a diameter of 10 kilometers. The ring's body would be two kilometers thick with the outer shell consisting of 500 meters of rock or concrete. Interior composition would be material collected from asteroids. The ring would be segmented into 31 pieces with water 20 – 25 meters thick in between each piece acting as a cushion and lubricant. A sleeve-disc combination would be placed surrounding the space between two segments. The pressure between each segment should be high enough to keep the water from 1) freezing and 2) boiling. The segmentation would allow for the ring to expand, contract, and warp (to a small degree) without damaging the ring as a whole. Each segment would contain dozens of spheres made of rock, concrete, or metal. Each sphere would house huge populations of people, animals, vegetation, life-support, and equipment.

Gravity within each sphere would be produced by centrifugal force. The Spheres would be divided into banded areas at different axis and latitudinal lines. The banded areas would rotate a different speeds, depending on their latitudinal location to create an equivalent of .5 to 1 Earth g.

The added benefit of the gyroscopic forces generated by the bands would help each segment maintain position within the ring assembly.

## Problem Statement

**There are a few** problems to consider with constructing and maintaining a mega-project such as the Carhayaken Ring:

- Materials gathered
    - Where?
    - How much is needed?
- Construction technology
    - Will current disciplines work?
    - Adapting terrestrial hardware to extraterrestrial use?
    - Efficiency and how much is good enough?
- Personnel
    - Skill level of workers?
    - More reliance on automation?
- Transportation technology
    - Current Rocket Science?
    - Advance Propulsion?
- Life support technology
    - Air generating?
    - Farming?
- Emergency preparedness
    - Containment breach?
    - Water and Air contamination?
- Ring assembly integrity and Movement
    - Allowing for flexing and uneven gravitation and inertial forces?
    - Orbiting transfers?

## Solution

**The ring segments** will be created from materials gathered from the asteroid field. Once we overcome the technological hurdle of capturing and transferring asteroids to different orbits, we can start constructing the ring. Current construction techniques should work and can easily be transferred to off-world construction.

Equipment will have to go through some developmental stages for adaptation for vacuum operations, personnel will have to be trained and properly equipped. Current screening procedures for astronauts will have to be greatly revised. Safety protocols will have to be revised, as well, accommodating mid-level skilled workers and there will be more reliance on robotic technology.

Today's rocket technology is currently adequate, however, for efficiency in material delivery and transportation we will have to start using more exotic propulsion systems such as ion drives and VASIMR systems. Time to complete a Carhayaken Ring is irrelevant, however, more advanced technology will be employed when it becomes available.

Once a ring segment has been completed, interior building should immediately commence. Each segment should be self-sustaining with power, water, propulsion, and life-support. Power will be generated initially from nuclear sources and then, eventually, switched to 100% photovoltaic and supplemented with battery storage. Population will be housed in large spheres embedded in each segment. Water will also be stored within each segment, but also can be drawn from the water section between each segment in the event of an emergency. Propulsion of each segment will mainly be used for attitudinal control and helping with initial orbital transfers.

Most segment control functions will have to rely on automation. Computers and robotics will control critical mission functions such as life-support, segment position control, power distribution, system repair, and orbit position. Humans would assist in final component assembly and wiring. Most system programming and monitoring will be done by humans. Cooking, some cleaning, some system maintenance and repair, furniture construction, and customizing of creature comforts will also be done by humans.

Initially, food, air, and water will have to be shipped to the first segment during construction. Afterward, all life-support needs can be supplied from the completed Segment One installation. The majority of water will be supplied from captured asteroids and comets. All necessary building materials will originate from captured asteroids. Propulsion fuel may come from Jupiter, Saturn, the other large planets, and a by-product of electrolysis for creating oxygen from water..

The propulsion system for each segment will consist of several components: Gyroscopic, Chemical, Ionic drive, and VASIMR systems. Positional stability will be maintained by the gyroscopic forces produced from the Population Spheres within each segment. Also, each segment would have a main command "deck" and Engineering section to control and monitor all functions and features of each segment. One Segment, in concert with the other segments, would control the entire ring assembly.

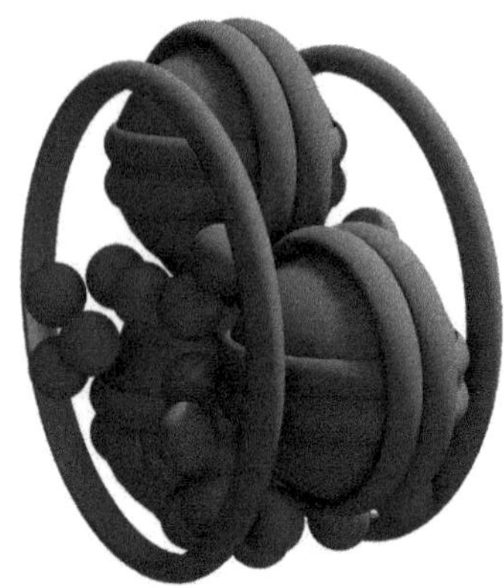

Segment habitat, work spheres, and Storage

Emergency Preparedness will consist of individuals carrying a container of emergency air at all times during the initial interior construction phase of each segment. Because each segment is covered in a thick shell of concrete, radiation exposure will be at a minimum. The Nuclear power generators would be maintained on the outer most portion of the segment and could be jettisoned in the event of an inevitable meltdown. Most emergency power needs could be supplied by photovoltaic systems so the loss of a nuclear power generator in a given section

of a segment would be negligible overall. A segment could also burn liquid fuel such as hydrogen.

LEED techniques would be established as an integrated normal practice throughout the build out phase of each segment. During the first few years of a segment being inhabited, emphasis on efficiency and energy saving would be placed when necessary. Each housing unit within a given segment would be supplied with emergency air, food, and water for several years. Training in fire suppression and atmosphere breach repair would be taught at different levels. All workers would be required to go through the basics. Once families are introduced and established, basic Emergency Preparedness, Safety, LEED, and Emergency procedures would be integrated into all levels of education.

Air generation will rely on a number of processes. Farming, traditional and other means, along with park and natural environments would be established. Vegetation within these designated areas would be used as a natural filter for scrubbing out CO2 and supplying oxygen throughout the segment spheres. Electrolysis for energy generating would also generate oxygen as a by-product.

As mentioned earlier, gyroscopic forces generated from Spheres needing to simulate gravity will help maintain overall ring integrity. The Sleeve-Disc combination pieces will allow for some movement along the y- and z-axis of each segment. Different Advanced Propulsion Systems will be used to fine tune segment position and when used in combination of other segments help with ring orbit transfer.

# Conclusion

**Potentially, Earth's overall** technological knowledge seems to be at a level high enough to undertake constructing a modest Carhayaken Ring. New exotic alloys will not be needed nor would radical building techniques have to be developed. Adapting current terrestrial construction methods to extraterrestrial usages would not require extraordinary measures. Getting International cooperation would probably be the most difficult. We already have several companies pursuing Asteroid mining and there are more than enough civilian companies capable of conceiving, developing technology, building equipment and tools, and launching everything, including people, into space.

---

## Related Work

Dyson sphere
https://en.wikipedia.org/wiki/Dyson_sphere

What is a Dyson sphere?
http://earthsky.org/space/what-is-a-dyson-sphere

Dyson sphere: What are the odds of an alien megastructure blocking light from a distant star?
By Anders Sandberg
http://www.ibtimes.co.uk/dyson-sphere-what-are-odds-alien-megastructure-blocking-light-distant-star-1525042

How to build a Dyson sphere in five (relatively) easy steps
http://www.sentientdevelopments.com/2012/03/how-to-build-dyson-sphere-in-five.html

What is a Dyson Sphere?
by FRASER CAIN on SEPTEMBER 19, 2013
http://www.universetoday.com/104919/what-is-a-dyson-sphere/

Torus
From Wikipedia, the free encyclopedia
https://en.wikipedia.org/wiki/Torus

Centrifugal force
From Wikipedia, the free encyclopedia
https://en.wikipedia.org/wiki/Centrifugal_force

Rotation around a fixed axis
From Wikipedia, the free encyclopedia
https://en.wikipedia.org/wiki/Rotation_around_a_fixed_axis

Gyroscopes
http://www.gyroscopes.org/behaviour.asp
http://www.real-world-physics-problems.com/gyroscope-physics.html

Asteroid Mining
http://www.planetaryresources.com/
http://www.space.com/30213-asteroid-mining-planetary-resources-2025.html

Water in Space
https://medium.com/starts-with-a-bang/does-water-freeze-or-boil-in-space-7889856d7f36#.qi7aq4llv

VASIMR
https://en.wikipedia.org/wiki/Variable_Specific_Impulse_Magnetoplasma_Rocket
https://www.youtube.com/watch?v=GIg6pWwezEU
http://www.adastrarocket.com/aarc/VASIMR

ION Drive
http://www.nasa.gov/centers/glenn/about/fs21grc.html
http://nmp.jpl.nasa.gov/ds1/tech/ionpropfaq.html

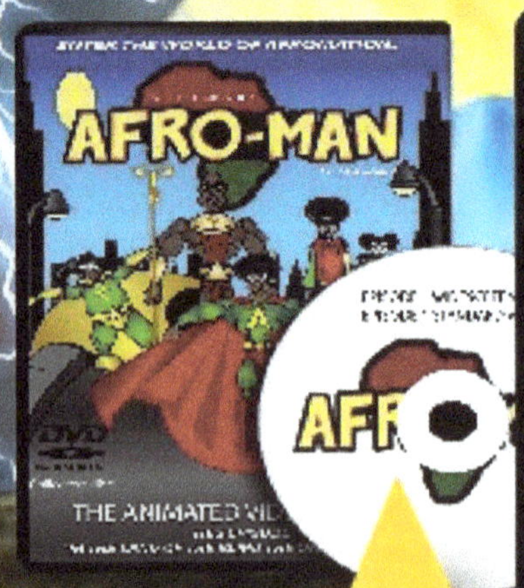
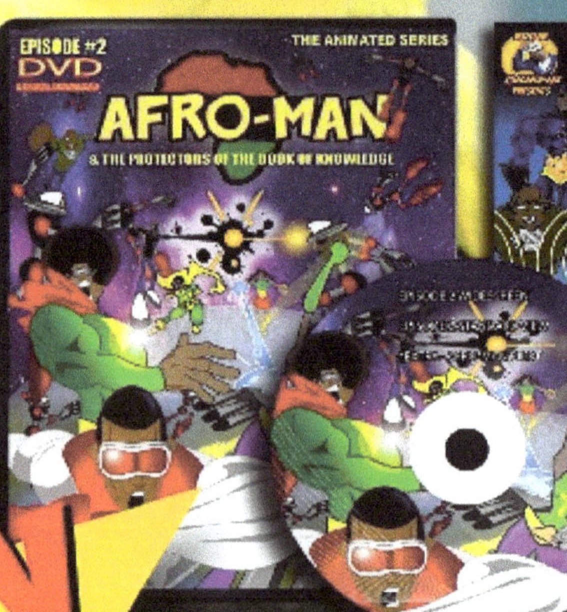


AFRO-MAN
AND THE PROTECTORS OF THE BOOK OF KNOWLEDGE
FUN FOR THE ENTIRE FAMILY!
KNOWLEDGE IS POWER!
AFRO-MAN
EPISODE #2
DVD
THE ANIMATED SERIES
AFRO-MAN
& THE PROTECTORS OF THE BOOK OF KNOWLEDGE
AFRO-MAN
FOR AGES 5 to 10
BUY NOW!
THE ANIMATED SERIES
WWW.AFROMANKIDSSPACE.COM

# BENEATH RED TAIL WINGS

## PART 2

### Patricia I. Williams

**William was confounded.** Where was he? He felt too weak to call out for Frances Ann. For a moment he believed Sarah was singing softly to him. Why were they here? He left them both safe, at the ranch. Where was this place? He returned to darkness. The pounding ache couldn't follow him there.

Sarah choked back tears. She wouldn't give up hope. For a moment it appeared her father would awaken. His eyes opened, but he never focused on anything. He grunted in pain and blacked out again. It was a good sign wasn't it? She wished Gil would hurry. Once more she began to pace back and forth, agitation growing. Tears began to flow unrestrained.

Oh, the one thing she had not done since the night she left home was to pray. Standing there in the shadowed doorway she bowed her head, thanked God for sparing her father's life and for His help to get them safely home. A deep breath held and released signaled renewed determination. Sarah checked her sidearm and walked outside looking around for Kevin.

Her momentary lighter heart was replaced with irritation when she realized his horse was gone.

"I don't believe you're still trailing Matt around. Kevin Harlan you have to be the most hard headed man I've ever met!"

Where was he when she was supposedly in danger. Was he protecting her father? Standing guard anywhere? No he was riding around in territory he didn't know and would probably get lost, again! He might never find his way back at all. Really, this was all so ridiculous.

*****

Kevin fumed while his pony picked its way through the thick brush. He had been watching that saddle bum real close. Contrary to what these cowboys believed, he wasn't a fool. The man had eyes for Sarah, oh yes he did. It wasn't going to happen, he'd make sure of that. Women were always taken in by penny dreadful, strong silent types, the unattainable ones. Where he came from all the silly girls thought cowboys were such heroes. They didn't see the reality; unwashed bodies, dung covered boots and chewing tobacco. Kevin wasn't going to remain here. He already invested too much time on this enterprise, but Sarah had been an unexpected bonus. She was stubborn as a mule alright enough. But when he did get a kiss, the feel of those womanly curves charged through him like lightening.

It would have been easy if the broken down bastard had stolen the money. Why hadn't he? Maybe he wasn't as down on his luck as it appeared. That Winchester was in mint condition, even he could see that. The man hadn't been wearing a sidearm when they got there, but after they settled in with him, it was soon hanging off his hip. It looked new too, not the battered relics most of the cowhands wore. He even slept with it on. Then Travers comes in claiming he's sick and Sarah went all soft hearted on him again. Didn't she know a man like that wouldn't want her pity? That girl was supposed to look all doe eyed at him, not some ragged wretched bastard! Oh, if only he knew what the man's game was. Why didn't the fool cut and run with that money? Why? He couldn't afford to have Sarah's head turned. There must be some way to make the man show his true intentions.

Damn it, all the stupid trees looked the same. Had he wandered off the trail? Travers should be just ahead of him. Sarah would be really angry if he got lost again. Kevin turned his mount around, unsure of his destination. Upset was the least of it now. His horse whinnied, causing him to jerk on the reins in surprise. A distant response gave him the general direction, but his mount moved off on its own. It was with no little relief the young man returned to the cabin, managing to elude the hard eyed young lady tapping her foot in the doorway.

He stalled his return indoors, reluctantly wiping down his pony. This is why cities had livery stables. Sarah would readjust to a life of refinement once they were away from here. The charming lady he met in Boston would once again come to the fore. No more camping trips, no snakes and slain carcasses hanging from trees. A carriage ride around the commons would certainly be more romantic than that filthy excursion, complete with unwashed cowhands and blood.

Out here, the hired help were too familiar with Sarah. The men praised her roping technique of all things, then scolded her when some chore was forgotten. What on earth was her father thinking allowing Sarah to herd cattle and rope steers? She even cleaned the stables and other disgusting activities. It also didn't help the fools thought his 'tenderfoot' status a source of hilarity. The jokes were stupid and insulting. Little did they realize he would have the last laugh. They would be looking for work and Boston would once again be his playground.
*****

Matt rode in with a stiff wind stirring up behind him. The temperature had dropped suddenly. There would be more rain, or worse an early snowfall. He looked forward to none of it stuck in a cabin with a wounded man and his family. Cobby was side stepping and snorting every time the eddies stirred his mane. It didn't take him long to wipe the old horse down and leave him to snap at the wind between cropping the scant foilage. He had just reached out to open the door when it slammed open

and Harlan stormed past him, red in the face and scowling. Matt tried to calm his racing heart and let go of his gun. He could have shot the young fool. The boy was absolutely oblivious to his surroundings. It could get him killed. Just the thought made Matt's temper rise. He stepped inside to find Sarah tight lipped and furious. He avoided her stare and raised chin by crouching before the fire and adding more fuel to it. The broth had boiled down, so he added more water.

"Kevin tried to follow you."

There was no follow up to the comment, so Matt turned to look at Sarah. The question was in the angle of his head. His eyes were obscured once more by his spectacles.

"He's suspicious of you and thinks you have other motives. He attempted to follow you, I should say. He got lost.

"I wasn't trying to hide where I was going. I would have been long gone and your father's body still on that ledge if I had wanted money. I have things I need to be seeing to and this has delayed me. Another storm maybe moving in on us and I..."

Matt stood up, suddenly speechless with rising anger and frustration. He directed a hard stare at Sarah and stalked out of the cabin. She was startled but took off after him. A fight with Kevin was not a good idea. Only there wasn't any confrontation. Matt once again disappeared into the forest. Sarah wondered how much more of this she could handle. Kevin was being an ass and Matt's abrupt departures and silence irritated her to no end. Fuming, Sarah realized her impotence in the situation. Perhaps the women clamoring for the right to vote and make decisions usually reserved for men had it right. All this bullheadedness was driving her around the bend.

Two hours later Sarah's mood took a lighter turn, when her father's eyes opened. She spoke softly to him, easing his agitated movements. She rushed to spoon some of the broth into his mouth, elated when he appeared surprised and swallowed it. She sang to him until he appeared to fall asleep. He hadn't looked directly at her but the sound of her voice did seem to calm him. She was determined this was a good sign. Another hour passed without a sign of either of her errant protectors. At least she knew Matt was around, because his wall eyed mount snapped at her when she went to see if he was still there. She laughed in relief.

Matt returned to the cabin with the ever present rabbits dangling from his hand. There seemed to be an excessive amount of the creatures. Good in this situation, but Denver was beginning to look better and better for the winter. He called out to the occupants of the cabin before approaching the door. He had been away for some time and Harlan may have returned. If Harlan was suspicious of him, getting shot would be too likely. Matt shivered inside his coat and the rising wind actually pushed him through the door when Sarah called his name. She was alone. Where was that fool? If he got himself lost in the woods again, Matt wasn't going to go looking. Not even if Sarah asked. No absolutely not. With a grimace he hung the rabbits over the grate, took off his coat and built up the fire. It wasn't long before the meat was roasting. He had made it a point to avoid Sarah's gaze, unsettled by his attraction to her. He didn't need this, especially since that puppy was so determined to let Matt see he had a claim.

Sarah sat on her bedding watching Matt cook the meat. He dropped some greens into the broth and added more water to it. He never said a word or looked in her direction. The quiet made her uncomfortable, but if he was still angry about Kevin perhaps this once she would leave it be. Rain began to fall in a steady patter. Just as she thought to go call out for Kevin, he charged through the door, looking shocked when Matt's gun snapped up to cover him.

"Mr. Harlan, you should call out before you come in, considering the circumstances."

"...Uh...uh, you're right Matt. I wasn't thinking. Wasn't expecting the rain..."

Matt's stare was hard and accessing for a long moment. Then his gun slipped back into the holster on his hip. He turned back to the fire to watch over the food. Kevin kept one eye on the man has he went to his bedroll and sat down beside Sarah. She was obviously still angry at him. His smile didn't soften her this time. She frowned and turned away, fussing with the blankets on her father's cot.

The remaining hours were tension filled as Kevin's attempts at conversation were not acknowledged. Sarah probably told Matt he was under suspicion. That would explain the gun when he walked in. The man hadn't been that guarded before. Damn, this would make things more difficult. They ate the wild greens and rabbit without comment and Matt cleaned up the area, all the while ignoring them.

"I, I forgot to mention, but my, my father woke up this afternoon."

Kevin twitched at her side, his face blank for a moment. Then he turned to her with his dazzling smile.

"Why that's fantastic Sarah, honey. Did he say anything? Any clue to who attacked him?"

"No, no he didn't speak at all. But he had a few sips of broth and then he went back to sleep."

Her expression was full of hope and lit up with her smile. Kevin took her into his arms and hugged her.

"Oh Sarah, that's great. See I told you he would pull through. It won't be long before we're home and this misadventure will be behind us."

"Thank you Kevin. I hope so I do."

She couldn't hold back her tears and Kevin pressed his wrinkled bandana into her hands. Matt watched them interact, but said nothing. He acknowledged her information with a nod. She didn't know whether to be angry or not at his lack of verbal response. She returned Kevin's kerchief and tried to keep the frown from her face as he squeezed her hands a little too tight. Without any more comment, Sarah got into her bedding and tried to sleep.

Harlan and Matt didn't speak again until Kevin made ready for bed.

"Mr. Travers...uh Matt...look I'm sorry alright? I guess Sarah told you I was trying to follow you around today. I, I don't actually know what to say about that. I'm sorry to be, but well, I never felt for anyone before like I do Sarah and well, she, I mean I want her to see me as well..."

His speech trailed off into silence, his beseeching gaze directed at the blank features of the scarred cowboy. The silence held for a too long moment. A frown twisted Matt's features before he sighed heavily.

"This isn't the city Harlan. Things a man does tells more than what he says. I have business of my own. Once the old man is back with the cowhands you and your girl will be on your way, and I will be on mine. That will be the end of it."

Matt went to his bedroll and stretched out. He left Kevin staring at him in consternation. So this man was just going to ride away without reward of any kind? No money, not even a job? Kevin rolled up in his own blankets listening to the annoying plonk, plonk plonk of water leaking from the ceiling. The old man had woken up, that could pose a serious problem. Sarah was real resistant to his attentions today. How could she stay mad for so long? He needed to think. What could he do about all this? His ruminations provided no answers and late into the night he dozed off.

The sun never broke through the clouds heavy with rain. Matt woke to gray shadows. He slept poorly during the night, disturbed by his continued confinement and the cannon shot thunder overhead. The room was damp and very chilled. Matt considered his options, but leaving a wounded man and a woman helpless didn't sit well. Tired of his indecision he dozed off, twitching now and then as the thunder continued to echo around the mountains.

It was just as dark when Matt woke again, but he rolled out shivering in the damp. After building up the fire, he broke his fast with a cup of the wild greens. Harlan woke, ignored him and staggered out into the rain. He came back wiping his face and hair down.

"Morning Travers."

"Harlan."

Kevin pulled a leg off the rabbit hanging over the fireplace, squatted by the fire and ate. No more was said. He occasionally glanced at Matt, but flushed and looked away if their eyes connected. Matt found this annoying, but was determined he wasn't going to get more involved with the irritating easterner than he already had. The chill in the air was increasing so the warmest place was directly before the fire. He may have to ride the trail and find the old man and

his hands. It would be best if this rescue happened before they were trapped. Putting on coat, slicker and guns he left the cabin.

Cobby was in a real disagreeable mood and attempted to bite him more than once. Matt didn't win the stare down with his soggy mount this time. He had to admit his efforts were halfhearted. The idea of slipping and sliding down the mountain and ending over a cliff didn't sit well with him. He finally left Cobby and the other ponies beneath the overhang behind the cabin and hoped the storm passed quickly.

Sarah was awake when Matt returned. She was picking over a bit of meat, leaning against the cot. It was obvious she was avoiding any interaction with Harlan and himself. After removing his slicker and coat, Matt settled onto his blankets. Another blast of thunder startled the occupants. Matt sat, one hand clutching the blanket and the other his sidearm. The sounds of cannon continued to echo and vibrate the leaky timbers. He couldn't stop the minute twinges that gripped his muscles under the assault. He hoped no one noticed his trembling hands, when he took the short strips of leather and rope from his bag. Soon he was lost in the rhythm of weaving his Solomon knots. The low light didn't obstruct his efforts. His fingers knew the task even when his mind was lost to the battlefield.

Lightening, thunder and pounding rain curtailed any conversation. The trio sat, damp and sullen throughout the dreary day. Mr. Bethancourt roused once. He appeared to be attempting to sit up, but Sarah soothed him and managed to spoon some broth into his mouth. He was conscious enough to swallow, but the strength to speak seem to have eluded him. Realizing she wasn't a dream accounted for his agitation. He was a very protective man. His wife and daughter never left the ranch without him or Gil riding escort. Gradually exhaustion caught up with him and despite his desperate denials, he was asleep once more.

*****

Matt lay in his blankets listening to the water still leaking from the ceiling. The rain seemed to have stopped for now anyway. He was cold. Tossing the blankets aside, he lurched to his feet and stretched. It took a few minutes to ease cramped muscles which had stiffened attempting to protect him from each explosion of cannon. His sweat and the dampness made his clothes adhere to his skin. With a grimace, Matt made his way to the door and stepped outside. The sun was blazing as if the rain never happened, so he dug out his glasses and hooked them over his ears. Squinting against the glare from sun lite puddles, he went into the trees.

After taking a moment to wash up at the rivulet, he leaned against the stone breathing deeply. He was damned tired. They couldn't stay here and expect the old man to survive the deprivations. But to get him off this mountain seemed impossible. Harlan would be useless on the trail considering he couldn't read sign or handle a horse very well. Matt didn't know what to do about this. If there were bad men out there, they had to be long gone by now. Better to chance leaving than to do without supplies. Old Gil could have had an accident or met with foul play. They didn't know and seriously couldn't wait. Frustrated he wrestled with the pros and cons.

Sarah checked her father over for the hundredth time. Maybe they could build a travois to get him off the mountain. But further exposure to the weather would probably worsen his condition. She would ask Matt about it. Uncle Gil should have been back, but then the weather would have caused the men to take shelter if at all possible. Maybe they would get there today. Originally Uncle Gil planned for them to ride back to the base camp if they hadn't found sign of father. She thought their worries were almost over, if only he would ride in right now. Sighing, Sarah tucked her father in and stirred up the fire. After adding more wood, she stepped out to attend to her private needs.

The scent of wet pine invigorated her, despite the chilled air. She skipped over puddles and shivered when icy water slipped past the collar of her jacket. Water splashed off the rim of her sombrero. Unconsciously Sarah's spirit was lifted. She used her bandana to freshen up, dipping it a deep puddle of icy water. It was a momentary energy, however. Kevin's

actions still irked her. When they got home, he would need to return to Boston. He was not functioning well in this crisis and she honestly couldn't see pursuing a relationship when he wasn't solid enough for this life.

Despite his talk of the city, Sarah could not see living the restricted life there. She hated every moment of her time spent at school. The first thing she had done when she returned home was saddle up her most rambunctious pony and ride as if the devil was after her, all over the range. She was stinking of sweat and half asleep from exhaustion when she got back. To her mother's consternation, she entered the house swearing loudly to never leave Colorado again, ever. She easily recalled her father's happy laughter when he wrapped her in one of his rib cracking bear hugs. Poor mother, she still didn't understand her wayward child.

The sun was warming her up as Sarah trekked back to the cabin. Her pleasant mood faded when she saw Kevin preparing to ride away from the cabin.

"Kevin! What on earth do you think you're doing?"

The pony spun on his heels, Kevin hauling on the reins. Something fell from the saddle into the mud. Furious, Sarah ran forward to give the idiot a piece of her mind. She was brought to a halt by the appearance of Kevin's sidearm aimed in her direction.

"Stop right there Sarah honey."

Kevin was holding a gun on her. She watched as he stepped down, watching her closely and groped around until he pulled her father's moneybelt from the mud. Spurred by outrage Sarah once more charged forward.

"How dare you! Have you lost your mind? You won't get away with this."

"Stop! Don't take another step. You wouldn't want me to shoot you now, would you?"

Kevin was standing tall, arm straight and gun steady in his hand.

"I was going to fight for you, honey. If those two tramps had done their job, I would have married you. You would have never known. But then I noticed some things. How eager you were to defend that saddle bum. How you didn't want my kisses anymore, always chasing after him. Did you lift that silly looking skirt for him this morning? Did you! It makes me mad. You want a broken down blind man over me! Oh yes, that's right, you don't know the tramp is going blind. Ha, ha look at Miss Bethencourt's face!"

Sarah was trembling with shock. What tramps? What was he talking about? This couldn't be happening. She forced herself to swallow, mouth dry and tongue cleaving to the roof of her mouth.

"Tell, tell me you didn't hurt father? Is, father..."

"Shut up, damn it. The old man didn't even wake up. He's dying anyway. Come to think of it those ranch hands are sure to be upset to find you dead out here with your old man. They might just hang that raggedy begger you're mooning over. Yeah, I like that idea."

"Kevin don't, don't do this."

"Kevin, don't do this," he simpered before pulling the trigger.

Sarah screamed, but it was Kevin's body folding over and falling to the ground. The shot seemed to repeat itself for an eternity to the woman's stunned senses. He said "I love you." He tried to kill her. Feet pounded the mud and one arm waved in the air scrabbling for purchase on nothing. Finally all movement ceased. Sarah continued to watch the body as if it was a rattler poised to strike. She didn't react when Matt moved passed her to kick Kevin's gun aside.

"See to your father girl. Now!"

Sarah shook all over and ran into the cabin. She hurried to lift her father back onto the cot. His upper body was almost over the side. She was further shocked when he groaned and murmured her name. The bandages around his shoulder were displaced, faintly stained with new blood. She rushed to clean the wound and cover it over with a clean bandana from her bag. After making him comfortable, she held his hands tightly, so grateful they were both still alive.

Eventually Sarah spooned the remnants of the broth into his mouth. Her joy when he finished the cup and smiled, battled with her other reactions to events. There were episodes of panic when breath would be lost, heart beating wildly. Then she would be fine again, if you discounted trembling hands and intermittent tears.

*****

A muscle twitched in Matt's jaw as he looked over the remains. Kevin's wallet was pretty flat. He wondered why the easterner didn't possess more than a comb and a creased, stained letter from Sarah dated a year ago. He laid them aside and turned the body over. The bullet entered just under Kevin's arm. Matt figured it broke bones then drilled his lungs and heart. There was blood in his gaping mouth, eyes wide, face flushed and swollen. He didn't die easy.

Matt knelt for a long time staring at the body. It could be Sarah's face with dead eyes and gaping mouth. He couldn't stop the gag reflex and heaved sour bile into the mud. After the army he swore never to kill another man. But he could not allow the girl to be killed. The writhing satisfaction in his gut was ruthlessly repressed. It wouldn't do to be happy the bastard was dead.

Before his thoughts got further lost considering motivations and guilt, Matt returned to the cabin and dug out his extra plate to dig a shallow grave. He hesitated when it came to the blankets. They may need Harlan's bedroll. No sense wasting them wrapping the body up. Sarah was sitting with her father, still teary eyed. There were no words he could think of to comfort her. He did check to see if her father was alright, quite surprised to find bloodshot eyes focused on him.

Standing around speechless wasn't going to accomplish anything. Squaring his shoulders, Matt went to bury the damned fool. It wasn't long before the repetitive effort to scour a trench in the damp soil settled his mind into the nothing which allowed him to face another day.

Sarah watched Matt come and go without a word. She busied herself putting the cabin in order. She went to the seep for more water, making an even thinner broth from the scant pieces of meat. Her father drank most of it. She told him what had been happening.

"I wish I could have warned you girl. I couldn't stop him. Two men tried to hold me up. I went for my gun. I don't, I don't remember anything after that."

"Oh, father! It sounds like Kevin sent those men after you. Did you know the men? Had you seen them before?"

"Worked on the ranch I think. Can't remember for sure," he whispered and closed his eyes.

"I don't understand why he would do such a thing? He was going to kill me and leave Matt to take the blame."

Sarah kissed her father's cheek, then pressed her ear to his chest just to hear his heart's rapid beating. They were alive! She was very grateful. Her prayer of thanks was interrupted by renewed tears. Exhaustion claimed her and she fell asleep. Will was not disturbed by his daughter's slumped form. They were not out of the woods yet. However, his frustration was not enough to overcome his wounded body's demand for rest. He slept.

Shadows pushed away the light inside the cabin as Sarah woke. She lit the fire and the lamp. She hadn't been sleeping very long, but her mind quickly turned to thoughts of Matt's well-being. He looked so sick when he came inside. It took more than a moment for her to realize the plate was being used to bury Kevin. They would be dead for certain if not for him. There could be no effort spared to make him see how grateful they were.

Her father moved restlessly until she sooth his anxiety with her presence. She kissed him on the cheek.

"Tell me about this man. The one I saw before. You say he found me?"

"He went out to bury Kevin. I'm worried father. He looked ill. I thought he might faint away. He said he brought you off a ledge and found this cabin, patched you up. Oh he was so protective. We had to prove who we were before he lowered his rifle. Even then he kept us under the gun. He never touched the money! It was lying right next to you and the latches hadn't been touched! Who would resist such a temptation? Even Uncle Gil was surprised."

"Well, I owe him. I owe him big and I'll see to it Sarah don't worry none."

"Dad, you know you always told me never

settle for less than a man I could respect. Well, Matt is...he is. I think I found him." Her eyes filled with tears again at ther declaration.

"Sarah," her father groaned and shook his head, "you were nearly engaged to that idiot easterner and he was no good. Don't start talking about any more fiancés, I won't live through another one, I won't."

"Oh dad I..." Sarah had the grace to blush red and covered her hot cheeks. "Get some sleep. Gil should be back today. We can go home."

"I can't wait," he mumbled. "Wake me when he gets here."

Sarah smiled and pulled the blankets to his neck tucking him in. She stepped out of the room, breathing deeply of the mountain air. They were alive, thank God. Matt was here and they were safe. As she thought of him Matt stepped around the corner of the cabin.

"I unsaddled his horse. Come morning we get going whether Gil is back or not."

"Yes, I think so too. Dad's able to talk now. The men who tried to rob my father were former hands."

Matt frowned at that.

"Lucky for him they made due with his horse and rig instead of going for the money. But we don't have enough ammunition to hold them off if they do show up again. Harlan claimed to be following me around, but there's no way to know what he was doing out here."

"Well, anything, anything at all you have it. I, we we're grateful Matt."

Sarah managed to look up into his eyes. She levered up and kissed his cheek.

Matt stepped away and frowned at her.

"Get inside and see to your father," he snapped.

Her eyes filled with tears again, but that didn't soften Matt. He turned away and disappeared into the trees, again. After the shocks of the day, this obvious rejection brought a fresh round of tears.

Matt could hear her sobbing, so he walked faster.

Sarah didn't know how long she stood

clutching the door frame and crying. It was so humiliating. He probably thought she was the most spoiled, fickle and callous woman alive. Dad was right, she didn't know her own mind and she was courting disaster once again. Obviously Matt found nothing attractive about a girl who could kiss him after he'd killed her near fiancé. Sarah's face flamed in shame again. She went inside and shut the door firmly behind her.

Matt held his head under the trickle of water using his bandana to scrub the worst of the filth from his body. It was cold, but he was sure there was still blood mixed with the mud on his hands. He gagged and retched for a long time. His chest and stomach burned when he managed to stagger back to the water. He rinsed his mouth and washed again. Alone, no one could witness his weakness. He cried, an awkward process that did not ease his disgust. If he hadn't killed Harlan two people might have died. He could have been digging Sarah's grave. He shivered continuously as he dressed and shrugged into his coat. He had no choice to go back and snub that girl. It was a kiss on the cheek, didn't mean anything but he, he didn't dare think. He was broken and no good would come of it.

Sarah was there looking vulnerable and frightened of him as he walked in.

"Miss Bethencourt, I apologize for my rough manner. I was out of line."

"I owe you the apology, Mr. Travers. I am not normally so ill-mannered and, and forward. I can only think the stress of the day... I ask your pardon."

Sarah stood by the fireplace wringing her hands as she spoke to him. Matt was watching the firelight glinting in her hair. She began to fumble at her skirt in confusion at his distraction. He finally tore his eyes away from her.

"I didn't mean to speak so harsh to you Sarah. I don't like killing a man."

He sighed.

"I'm tired girl. The ground was, ah I'm sorry. We better turn in. I'm too tired."

All he had to do was cross the room to his bedroll. It seemed a long way off.

"You haven't eaten. I..."

"I couldn't." The thought made him nauseous again.

"Some coffee?"

"No, no nothing. Just get to sleep."

He avoided her by walking to the other side of the table and kneeling beside his bedding.

She followed him and the muscles in his shoulders tightened at her hovering.

"I hope Kev...he didn't take anything."

"Take? What?"

"He said, he said he went through your things."

Matt spun on his heels and jumped to his feet.

"That bastard, I.."

Sarah and backed away, shocked by his reaction. Suddenly Matt's face was bleached of all color and he swayed as if struck. Sarah rushed forward and wrapped her arms around his waist.

"Matt, Matt what is it?" She staggered as his weight shifted again.

"Here sit, no no in the chair."

Matt fell into it and covered his face with unsteady hands.

Sarah ran to Kevin's saddlebags and dumped the contents on the floor. Her own hands shook as she found his silver plated flask and rushed to splash the brandy into a cup.

"Here drink this, drink it!"

She pushed his hands away from his face and pushed the cup to his lips.

"Drink it down!"

Matt grimaced at the taste but took the cup and drained it. Sarah watched him. He never looked up, but after awhile his color returned and his breathing slowed. The silence stretched.

She sighed. An owl hooted and swooped over the roof. One of the horses bumped the wall and snorted. Probably his.

"I better check around outside." Matt's voice startled her from where ever her numb mind had gone. Before she could say a word he was up and out the door.

He was gone so long she got nervous and placed her gun on the table.

Finally he stepped inside.

"Thank God." He looked surprised at her relief.

"Everything's alright. No signs of anyone around."

"Good. Would you sit down here for a minute Matt?"

He folded his arms and backed away from her.

"It's late Sarah. We need to sleep."

"You need to sit and hear what I have to say," she snapped. She surprised him again.

He approached the chair as if she was a threat and sat down.

Sarah took a deep breath.

"You have suffered more than inconvenience because you stopped to help my father. I'm sorry Kevin went through your belongs, but Matt, what he told me doesn't make any difference. I mean..."

"What did he say?"

"He...your eyes, that the doctors didn't know how long your sight might last."

Her voice was a whisper that screamed to him of pity. He clenched his fists in an effort to keep still and not scare her to death. If Harlan was alive right now, he would probably have killed him for this.

"...and I think you are just the bravest man I'ver ever met. Twice you have risked everything for strangers and I, I just wanted you to know..."

Suddenly she was on her feet and around the table. Before he could move her arms encircled his shoulders and she hugged him hard as she could. Matt wanted to get away but they were a vise stealing his breath and the strength from his body. Then his arms came up and wrapped around her waist. He was hugging her back. He turned his face away from the firelight into the soft darkness of her body. His throat ached and when he would have pulled away, her arms tightened. She laid her cheek against the tangled curls on his head and murmured, "It's alright", over and over again.

On the cot in the corner William Bethencourt listened as well as watched his daughter's grieving face. Sarah never could resist a wounded critter and it looked as if she really lost her heart to this one. The easterner never made her look so broken hearted even when he betrayed her and died.

Matt could not remember being so tired when he finally rolled up in his blankets. Across the room Sarah smiled and his heart beat faster. He smiled back then quickly covered his face with his hat.

Come morning, Matt found Mr. Bethancourt awake. He nodded at the young man so Matt went over to check his wounds. He helped him sit up in the bunk and drink some water.

"I intend to pack us out of here today. No sense waiting on your foreman. Something could have happened to him."

"Gil's an experienced hand in these mountains. But you're right anything is possible. I think it would be better if you rode down and brought the men back. Sarah says the camp was completely outfitted to look for me as long as it took. We could hold up here till I was better if they set up camp. Some of them could go on back and let my wife know we're okay. That trail is barely passable during wet weather. Gil and the boys might be trying to break a new trail to get here if there's been a landslide or something. If you can't get through turn back and we will manage, cause I know they won't stop till they make it. Try to shoot something other than rabbit and we'll be set." Will tried for a steely eyed glare, but he must have looked the fool because Sarah's giggle surprised both the men.

Matt scratched his head and frowned.

"I don't like it."

"Neither do I but..."

"We may not have a choice." Sarah chimed in. She was sitting up in her blankets yawning and stretching. "Matt can check his rabbit snares and that should tied us over."

Will grunted.

"When we get home I'm telling Freida no more Hassenpfeffer. Don't care what she thinks we'll get another cook if we have to."

Sarah laughed. Freida was more likely to toss her father off the ranch than quite her job. Both her sons had worked the ranch and now had their own homesteads and families.

"A man's got a right to a decent meal. I don't know what you were thinking girl, but you are going back to the kitchen!"

Sarah's mouth fell open in outrage.

"No, no Mr. Bethencourt Sarah didn't cook the stew. That was me!"

"You tryin' to poison me boy?" Will peered at Matt through narrowed eyes.

In spite of his embarrassment Matt joined Sarah in laughter. Well, more like a big smile for Matt who rarely found reason to laugh out loud. Will's effort to hang on to his ire made Sarah laugh harder. It was some time before the raucous sounds faded.

Sarah finally strapped on her gun and excused herself. She returned to the cabin washed up and rebraiding her hair. Matt watched her from the corner of his eye during that process. Once she caught his gaze and smiled.

He loved her.

He sat on his bedroll cleaning and reloading their guns, his stomach growling from hunger.

He loved her.

Sarah noticed Matt was working really hard. The rag flew back and forth across his rifle as if it could shine brighter. When he finished he went off to check his snares, disappointed but not surprised to find them empty. The rain would have kept anything in the vicinity under cover.

"Stay close to the cabin. Keep your guns near at hand."

Will slipped his hand gun beneath his blankets.

"I'm still not sure about this Mr. Bethancourt."

"Well son, it's you or Sarah and I think she's safer here. Trying to get me off this mountain may kill us all. Besides I ain't eating any more rabbit. So ride out boy and be careful."

Matt shook Will's hand before hoisting his saddle to his shoulder. He left the cabin to do battle with Cobby. Sarah watched from the doorway, rifle in hand, while Matt saddled then went through the murderously intent exercise Cobby took to unseat him. When she judged it safe she stepped out to wish him well.

"Stay close Sarah. I'll be fast as I can."

"Don't worry about us. Watch the trail and take care."

With a nod Matt was gone. Sarah watched until she lost sight of him and returned to the cabin. Will was dozing when she got inside, so she freshened up the coffee, fretted over what she could scrap together for her father. She was sipping on the bitter liquid when shots were clearly heard. She paid no attention to the coffee splashing into the flames as he tossed the cup away in surprise.

She ran to her father's side as he struggled to push himself upright.

"Sarah, we got to stay together. You can't go out there after him. They might be waiting for just that."

"No dad, Matt..."

"I know Sarah, but he may have got them. If he didn't we still have to wait."

Sarah couldn't keep away from the window, however. She slid along the wall and tried to peek out for any sign of Matt. Her heart was beating so quick she was finding it hard to breath.

Endless minutes passed with no indication of what had happened out there, then suddenly she could see Matt's pony. Sarah sprang for the door, ignoring Will's weak sound of protest. If someone shot her now so be it, she could not leave Matt slumped there. Cobby stood just beneath the shadow of the trees at the edge of the clearing. She slowed to a walk and spoke softly as she called to Matt.

"Matt, Matt it's Sarah. Can you hear me? Matt can you..."

"The old man, oh damn Sarah the old man...," he gasped. She barely took in his words at the sight of the ragged hole in his coat.

Then he passed out and his pony snorted and shied away from her. She wasn't a fool to approach a spooked animal especially one as nasty tempered as Matt's.

"I just want to help him Cobby. Let me get Matt down," she continued to cajole and took another step. He bared his teeth and she stopped. The old man? No, no Uncle Gil would never! But what other old man could it be. Oh God, what if? The idea rocked Sarah's world completely off it's axis.

"Matt, Matt please you have to get off. I can't get to you. Please Matt wake up!"

A groan heralded Matt's return to consciousness.

"Matt get down."

"Sarah I, right. Down." And he slid from the saddle. Cobby snapped at the air and danced away from the body. She rushed to help him up, but he was dead weight.

"Sa-rah no, Will save Will. The old man after him," he gasped.

Matt grabbed her roughly with his good arm and shook her though he nearly passed out again. Gritting his teeth against the urge to vomit, he swore.

"Damn girl, your fa..." His face twisted horribly and he couldn't stop his body shutting down.

Sarah understood, she did. Though she was frantic for Matt she ran back to the cabin wondering why she was still alive if Gil had betrayed them. Did he think Matt was dead? Would he come here? Could her father kill him, could she? Was he watching? Did he think Matt was dead? There was no way he could have got to her father when she was right there.

Even so she was startled to see the door open. Gripping her sidearm, Sarah crept on and peeked in. Gil was holding a gun on her dad.

"Get in here Sarah honey. You won't be shooting me cause Will will take a bullet before I drop."

Gil was standing on the other side of the table away from the fireplace, his gun hand steady as always. Her father was propped up in bed as she left him. His face was pale and sweating. Their eyes must be the same, stunned by impossibility of this moment.

"This ain't no standoff Will. I'll shoot ya, no doubt."

"Why Gil? I don't understand? You and Harlan?"

"Why! You're sayin' you don't know why? I broke my back for you. Helped you make a fortune and what did I git? How many broken bones, freezing nights savin' your cattle, fightin' off rustlers. You name it I did it. Worked my tail off for you Will. What did I git?! And then this half breed lookin' devil comes along and saves your hide. You always had too much damn luck. And then he kills my son!"

Both Will and Sarah shouted in surprised denial.

"No Gil, tell me it ain't so. Harlan was your son? Why didn't you tell me? The boy..."

"You think when I found out I wanted him breakin' his back for a dollar a day? I spent all I had to make sure that woman took him back east to educate him for something better. We would have had it all and no one the wiser. Kevin was to marry her."

"Gil you know I would have helped you, you know that!"

Will couldn't believe what he was hearing. Harlan could have grown up on the ranch and gone back east to finish schooling like Sarah. They could have been brought up together, instead.

"Harlan wanted to kill Sarah, Gil. He wanted to kill her!"

Gil fingered the trigger guard back and that snapped Sarah out of her shock. She stepped forward. He ignored the gun in her hands, so sure of her.

"Uncle Gil. I can't let you hurt dad."

He never took his eyes off Will.

"This is between me and your pa, Sarah. I'll get to you soon enough."

Surely her heart stopped at the cold intention in that statement. This man had held her in his arms, rocked her to sleep many a night and taught her how to ranch and survive the rough life they led. How could he have hated them so much?

"I offered you part of my own ranch Gil. You could have made a home for your boy right here."

Will was praying Sarah would survive this. Gil didn't know about his gun, but the man was a good shot and he had Will dead to rights. They might both eat lead today.

"What the hell would I want with the ridge line. The grazing over there ain't half as good as you got. You think I would a been satisfied with your leavenings? Stake me with cattle you don't want? When ya went into business with them miners, ya didn't offer any of that!"

"You know I loaned them money when they had none. No one knew they would make a big strike.

You told me yourself you thought I was throwing money away after dreamers. Remember it how it was Gil. You had your chances just like everyone else out here. If you were too scared to take the risks it ain't my fault!"

Gil flushed, enraged at the accusations. He glared at Sarah, daring her to shoot.

"Kevin wasn't much, but he was my flesh and blood. I seen you coolin' to him the last few weeks. I knew you was gonna change your mind. We decided to go for the money, only Kevin hired on those two lay abouts to do the deed and botch the damn job! But it's my time now."

Sarah's chin lifted. Nobody was hurting her dad today.

"No Sarah!"

Distracted by Will's shout, Gil's shot went wide and smashed into the wall. Will's gun discharged at the same time, burned through the blankets and struck Gil in the lower abdomen. Sarah's bullet smacked into his body just below his sternum. Desperate to stop him, she pulled the trigger again. Her father's shouting stopped her before she emptied her gun.

The air was thick with gun powder. Gil lay face up in the lamp light. Red stains spread across his shirt front. Sarah walked over to the body and stared for a moment. She bent on shaky knees, removed the gun from Gil's hand and backed away. She managed to look at her father and realized he was still alive. She just walked over and sat on the bunk taking his trembling hand in hers.

Sarah looked around the room. Matt's book lay on the table top where he left it before riding out. Her father's shout of surprise went unheeded as she rushed outside with a canteen, burning with fear that Matt had died because she was in shock. Cobby stood nearby suspicious eyes lock on his downed master. His ears pricked forward at her approach, but he didn't charge or snap. Quickly Sarah checked Matt over. His heart still beating. She wiped his face and begged him to wake up, so she could get him inside.

Still she was frightened when his eyelids fluttered open and there was a moment when he didn't recognized her or remember what had happened. She could see the confusion.

"It's alright now Matt. We stopped him. Gil's dead. It's alright."

He attempted to speak but didn't have the energy. She got him to take a few sips of water before she struggle to get him standing. It was a long difficult journey back to the cabin. He passed out once again, so she ran inside to get bandages to stop the bleeding as best she could. Maybe another hour went by before she managed to get him inside, then lowered him to his blankets she had laid out.

Her father lay quiet while she tended Matt. The bullet was still in his shoulder. It needed out but her hands were just too unsteady to do the deed at the moment.

"Sa-rah, thought he killed you, Sarah. Thought...glad glad you're not..."

"No Matt, father and I are both fine. Gil's dead. We...we both." She didn't try to hold back her tears. She still had to get Gil's body out of the cabin. None of them could sleep with his body there.

"Medicine, in my bag. Just a drop or two please, hurts Sarah." Matt choked back the urge to throw up. The pain was bringing back the memories of war and the ship.

"Yes, I remember. Just hold on Matt I'll take care of you. Don't worry."

It didn't take long to find the little bag with the tiny bottle in it. He was grateful for the dulling of his senses.

"Sarah, no more. No more even if I ask, promise," he whispered.

She frowned, but nodded agreement and Matt finally relaxed on the blankets.

"Sorry can't help, sorry."

She waited until he appeared to sleep, although there was a grimace now and then. First light she had to get that bullet out. This was all too much, but she wasn't done.

Despite her father's protest, Sarah managed to move Gil's body out of cabin. There was no way she could do anything else, so she left him there. She went back inside, barred the door and went to her blankets. Completely spent, Sarah laid down and slept. Her father lay much longer watching the two

young people sleep. He would probably never be able to tell how proud of her he was. Sarah was one to ride the river with, no doubt about it.
*****

Frances Ann Bethancourt paced the length of the porch shading her eyes from the noonday sun. Her daughter and the hands had gone looking for William nearly two weeks ago. First she worried, then she was terrified. For the past two days she had not slept or eaten. This morning she put on her dark gray Sunday dress and coiled her graying auburn hair tightly at the nap of her neck. The nights were very cold, the more so since William was not there to hold her. He was hurt on the trail or worse robbed of the money he carried, otherwise everyone would be back. She would rather be fussing over her stubborn man by now.

The door opened behind her and Frieda stepped out. The cook watched Frances pace before shaking her head in frustration. She sat down in one of the rocking chairs. Everyday Frances put on her prettiest dresses. This was a bad sign, this drab church going dress. Frieda sipped her coffee in silence. Frances' thin form moved back and forth, the numerous petticoats sweeping the porch. Her hands were twisting and knotting her handkerchief.

Both women lept to their feet when one of the stable hands came running from the barn.

"Their back, the boys are back. I could see Miss Sarah's sombrero from the loft."

He was pointing in the barn's direction which blocked the women's view of the distant mountains and narrow tree shrouded trails.

"Ya can't see 'em now Freddy. Almost to the house though."

The man ran back to the barn to make ready for the influx of exhausted horses. Men began to rush back and forth. Frieda put her arm around the frail bodied woman and held on.

"Oh Freddie what if..."

"None of that nonsense, you hear me. William is one strong mule headed man. He probably fell on his head and they had to tie him to the saddle!"

Frances laughed but it turned into a sob and she wept onto Frieda's shoulder. It was past time for the tears to fall. Now what ever had to be done, no matter how bad it was Frances would present a strong face by the time the party arrived. It was the longest two hours of their lives. Both considered the worst as the solemn group arrived.

Frances almost fainted when she realized William was mounted, but looking as if he wished he was not. Sarah smiled when she saw her mother and Frieda rush down the steps.

It was the cook who noticed the man strapped to a travois. Frieda had the men bring him into the quest room they kept aside for anyone seriously ill. She wondered where Gil was and that lazy easterner who had come to visit. Maybe the foreman had finally taken him to task. But that would be explained later, this young man needed tending bad and she sat to clean his wound and give him a thorough scrubbing.

When Sarah came in to help, Frieda took one look at her pinched wan face and chased her off to bed. For once William argued not at all to a hot bath and a long sleep beside his exhausted wife.

One of the hands was riding to see if the doctor was still at Wimbly's. Soon everything would be set right.
*****

Matt blinked, then turned his head away from the light. He attempted to go back to the quiet cocoon, but the banging of a tin pan snatched him into complete awareness. A moment more and it occurred to him he was resting on a real bed with flannel sheets and goose down pillows. A breeze stirred his hair, so he turned to see an open window. Curtains with a rose pattern lifted in the air. Voices drifted to him, talk of fences and stock, chores to be done.

He moved, becoming aware of bandages swarthing his chest and tying his left arm down. He experimented, moving parts of his body until he was sure all of him was there. He tried to remember how he got to this place, however fell asleep during the effort.

Matt's eyes opened again just as Sarah stepped through the bedroom door. Her face lit with joy at the sight of him?

"Matt, you're awake!"

He watched in amazement as the girl with copper hair crossed the room and planted a long kiss on his lips. She smelled like magnolia blossoms. Surely this was a dream.

Please, please let him stay here.

Sarah laid her beautiful head very gently on his good shoulder.

Matt realized he was delirious and didn't care at all. He inhaled deep as he could without pain to hold her essence inside.

"Sarah? Are you, is this real?" It's a wonder she heard the broken whisper, his throat was bone dry from fever and weakness.

"Oh yes, Matt. It's real."

"Where?"

"Home, Matt," she raised her head and gazed into his tired eyes. "We are home, understand?"

He sighed, content to let his eyes feast on her face for the moment. He would rest again and she would still be there.

"Yes," she whispered as if answering his unspoken thought. He didn't mind dreaming Sarah kissed him, even if his lips were cracked and sore.

Sarah listened to his heart's steady beat sooth her to sleep.

The End

Available online, at your local book store, or from http://mythicallegends.com

EXTRA ES SOLAR
MAELSTROM
ariel-x.deviantart.com

EXODUS EXTRASOLAR
ariel-x.deviantart.com

# Oreo - A little dog with a BIG problem

Oreo is a little dog with a big problem. He has a food addiction. Follow Oreo as he comes to understand his addiction and the steps he takes, not always successful, to control and overcome this affliction.

**Available at Amazon.com - For Kindle or in Print**

# Psyche
## A Story of Virtual Law
## Brandon Hill

for the weekend. Though there was never any real reason to take it off -nanomaterial could mimic any fabric and was self-cleaning, on some paranoid level, a part of her felt like she was not so much in control of it, as it was trying to take over, like she was in a constant battle of wills against the A.I. that governed its components. What worried her most was how it resisted whenever she did remove it, as if it hated her for rejecting the comfort and protection it provided. It felt like pinpricks in each of the pores of her skin, as if hanging on for dear life, making a conscious effort to remain on her, even after she gave the mental "release" command.

It was a fear she only shared with Dr. Galt, the League psych evaluator. What a coincidence that her train of thought would swerve in this direction during an evaluation. And no doubt Dr. Galt would pick it up, either on the brain scan running through her biocomp or on his own, being the off-planer and psychic that he was.

"Tried to sneak away from our little session again, have we?" The doctor asked in his slightly exaggerated, almost-German accent. The chief had to have told him about her previous attempts at shirking her appointments; it was the only way he could have known. She had hoped that she could have done so again, but the chief liked to keep a tight leash on his subordinates. The reminder popped in her field of vision today just as she had finished lunch: priority one, mandatory. The doctor was kind enough, but his voice, for its out-of-place accent, was oily, snake-like, and did little to endear him to her. But she bore him no ill will; after all, he did go out of his way to be nice.

"I hope it wasn't because of me." The doctor rubbed his tiny hands together as one of the four pseudopods that grew from his hunched back

**Today was Friday**, the end of her standby shift. This meant that Kate would be shuffling off her uniform manipulated the readouts upon the touch screen of his OffBoard peripheral.

"No. Not you," A flat, mildly sarcastic tone managed to escape her voice, even though she was being earnest. "You'll excuse me if I don't like you probing into my head."

"Oh, surely it's not so bad," Dr. Galt protested, with a laugh that was just as dissonantly unsettling as his voice. "Procedure and all that, especially when you've got so many bionics attached to you."

"Yeah. Procedure," Kate echoed, unable to move much more than her arm to bring the cup of Darjeeling tea to her lips. Tendrils of nanofiber ran like cascades of straight black hair from her uniform, wove together at their ends like braids, and were shunted into multiple jacks on several terminals. All there was left was to sit and wait while the doctor took his readings. "Thanks for the tea, by the way."

The doctor nodded cordially, and continued his work. No questions were asked; there was no need. He could see inside her mind as easily as he could see readouts from her OnBoard as it fed data into his brain via the INplant at his right temple. And this composed the entirety of the evaluation in all its inane boredom.

"Seems that everything is in order," the doctor said at last, stirring Kate from her state of between-sleep-and-awake. He touched a key sequence on his periphery, and the tendrils retracted from the terminals, flowing like a river running on rewind, into her suit's mass reservoirs with an audible snap. The empty teacup rattled in her hands upon its saucer. "And that will be all for me … until next month, that is."

With little more than a noncommittal sound, Kate rolled out of the couch. Her steps were ungainly at first, but her biocomp quickly compensated as it awoke from standby mode. She managed a brief smile at the doctor as she left the office, but had no intention of showing up next month. And to make sure that the chief would not call her out on it, she planned to have a talk with Jackie about the League mainframe, schedules, and the fudging thereof.

The ghost of an itch ran across her skin. She scratched reflexively. God, she would be glad to get this thing off, and move around without digital checks and balances made on her every bodily function! Now, there was only a brief detour for calibration and diagnostics, and then she would be home sweet home, enjoying beer and barbecue packs.

Kate paused, suddenly as a ping ran through her biocomp and caused a tremor in her skin. The words, PRIORTIY MESSAGE: REPORT TO DIRECTOR GARRETT, shone in bright red, flashing their urgency in her line of sight.

"Damn," Kate said under her breath. Had he started reading her thoughts now?

It was worse, she discovered all too quickly.

"Your regular shift has been extended." The director had said the words she dreaded. Her insides were one part a lead weight, and one part seething with vitriol. But she maintained a steady poker face; duty first, after all. It was always duty first with the League, but she could not help the thoughts that ran unbidden through her mind.

What the hell are you thinking?

Do you have any idea how much I look forward to taking this thing off?

Don't you have about a hundred other A-Class enforcers on tap?

"What's the assignment?" Was what she asked.

"The MAGI," Garrett said. "I'm sure you heard of them?"

With a thought, Kate's biocomp scoured the I-Link and supplied her with the relevant data about the organization. There was, surprisingly, very little. They were considered a terrorist group by the League simply because they opposed them (paranoid much?). Their list of "sins" consisted mostly of data infiltration and industrial espionage on some pretty sophisticated mainframes.

Kate frowned as her feelings of indignation deepened to something that was almost like hatred. This was grunt work, pure and simple, and far beneath an A-class. "What's wrong?" She asked, disguising her disdain under a veneer of snide stoicism, "techies can't handle a few super hackers?  Finally caught one in the real world, and you need me to babysit him?"

"No."

Oh, right.  Humor and sarcasm were completely wasted on the director.  His tone was as flat as yesterday's soda, colorless as his office: no plaques, pictures, or personal effects of any kind, save the League half-star symbol, mounted prominently behind him in brass behind his featureless mahogany desk.  The man was practically a robot.

He touched a sequence on his OffBoard, and Kate's biocomp signaled an upload with a shrill chirp.  Immediately, data integrated itself with her memories.

"Those are your orders," the director said with finality as a familiar name stood out the data.  The face to match that name suddenly came through the door, her blue skin and snow-white hair unmistakable.

"Mukai?"  Kate rose from her chair quickly to greet her friend.  "When did you come back to Earth?"

Mukai smiled kindly and bowed.  "An hour ago.  It is good to see you again, friend Kate.  I look forward to working with you."  She spoke in Glossiu, the language of her world, meaning her INplant had not been outfitted with an English translation matrix.  Her transfer to Earth had indeed been a swift one.

"She will be working with you on this case," the director announced.

"You're joking, right?" Kate quipped. Perhaps no English module was a good thing, she thought, or else Mukai might have taken her words as an insult.  She gave her a quick glance, but Mukai's decorum was better than a marine's.

"No.  She has the technical expertise you will need.  And you two have had a good, albeit brief working history, and a longer personal history.  You know this is a good pairing, Lieutenant."

"Krid," Kate swore under her breath. Robot though the director might have been, he was always right.

***

Their first stop was supposed to be at an ATM across town, but a real-time update had changed their destination to the old transcontinental Bridge: an abandoned project from the more optimistic previous century, where squatters had set up a miniature city over the years.  Apparently, a new suspected access had been made at a local restaurant that she was familiar with, but details, as expected, were sketchy.  Mukai had always been few of words, but she had obviously never driven a car through subspace; the way she flinched as the ghosts of traffic passed harmlessly through their car where there should have been lethal collisions was amusing, but not unexpected.  Subspace was the best way to travel if one were in a hurry.  Kate found herself unable to suppress a laugh as Mukai staggered out of the car onto the parking lot, making profuse apologies.  Kate reassured her friend that her disorientation was normal, and then led the way up to the shops, bazaars, parlors and dives on the Bridge's second tier.

"First time on enforcer business?"  Kate asked.  Though Mukai wore no English translation matrix, Kate had one for Glossiu, though she knew the language fairly well.  Still, a matrix helped for the big words.

"It is my first time directly working with one on Earth," Mukai said with a nod.

"Well, it's good to have someone helping, even if you're an import," Kate admitted.  "I mean I don't know what could've possessed the director to deputize an off-planer from a completely unrelated organization, but…" Her voice trailed off as they neared their destination down the crowded thoroughfare, its old sign suspended from overhanging rooftops.

That was when she realized that the sign was actually on.  The unusualness of this alone gave her pause to just stare.  The name "Pink's" shone in neon cursive, the same color as the name, as if it had never spent those last ten years burned out and unrepaired.

"Under new management it seems," Kate observed aloud, then saw that the windows of the facade had been repaired, and a fresh coat of varnish graced the entrance door.  Even the latch was new, shining with the near-gold sheen of polished brass, where the old one was rusted solid and had barely been hanging onto the door frame.

She stepped inside, and the unexpected and pleasant scent of newness and sawdust greeted her. The place looked like some itinerant fairy had taken up light housekeeping reversed the effects of time. The many and sundry photos of the music groups who played there in the past were still posted on the walls, but amidst a backdrop of fresh white paint newly applied to the sheetrock, free of yellowing and graffiti; the furniture, tables, menus and order terminals were also brand new.

"If I wasn't on duty…" Kate said. With a wistful sigh, she steeled herself for the task. ahead.

"We'll be checking the order terminals first," she told Mukai. After showing her credentials to the surprised, but acquiescent manager, she set to work.

During the investigation, Kate realized, much to her chagrin, that she was hungry – small wonder there, since the director hadn't given her the opportunity to grab a snack before heading out, and she was long overdue for dinner. And that the VIRsense matrix encoded into the order terminals for OnBoard access did not help to diminish her appetite. Soon, after being bombarded by the simulated sights and smells of a hundred menu items, she could stand no more. She jacked out of the system and located Mukai, who was now five rows down and still hard at work. I'll leave her to it, she thought, personally wanting to just get away from the torment of food.

She snapped the terminal's face plate back into place as her jack retracted back into her suit, then prepared to make an order for something to drink while the investigation continued, still decidedly, annoyingly unfruitful.

A minute later, she was sipping on a glass of iced Green Dream, inputting parameters of real world legwork into her biocomp. She was admiring the finished half of the ongoing repair job on the rear stage, when she noticed someone appear from behind the curtains.

"Hey!" Kate hurried down the way, and through the barricades that warned of the danger. "That's a microbot area; get out of there. You could mess up their programming; they might turn this whole Bridge into-"

She paused in her tracks as she approached the stage, and then slowed to a walk. A smile had erupted upon her face, as well as the face of the person across the way.

"Aly!"

"Sis!"

Kate's mind went back to a conversation with a coworker from about three years ago, and the photo that accompanied it, still hanging on the wall above the booths in the eating area. She had been right. Alicia did look almost exactly like her, but with shorter hair, highlighted in purple, and with a star tattooed beneath her left eye. It had been years since they'd seen each other, until they were reunited during an investigation in Mukai's home dimension of Gaia nearly two years ago. Kate's younger sister grinned as she sat on the edge of the stage, her legs dangling. She wore all black, and for a moment, Kate thought it was another enforcer uniform. But as her sister reached out and took her hands, and then hopped to the floor where they shared a happy embrace, she noticed that there were no line patterns or half star insignia - then it dawned on her that it was a diffusion suit, for safe interaction with on-duty microbots.

"Nice coinkeydink, meeting you here," Alicia said.

"I used to come here all the time, actually," Kate replied. I actually saw you perform a few times, back before you went platinum."

Alicia sighed as she ran her gaze across the breadth of the stage, the billions of microbots still hard at work, doing repairs one molecule at a time, un-rotting the wood, re-weaving and re-coloring the curtains, and un-rusting the metal. "Yeah, it brings back memories; that's for sure. Broke my heart when I came back from tour and saw the kridpile this place had become."

"Well then," Kate said, "if you're not the luckiest girl in all the worlds. Seems like the new owner liked this place the way it used to be."

Alicia gave a wry grin. "Who do you think bought it?"

Kate gave an explosive laugh that surprised even her. "You're kidding! "You bought this dump?"

"Won't be a dump for long," Alicia said. "Soon, this'll be the hottest night spot on the Bridge."

"No krid?" Kate scanned over the half-completed stage, a jarring contrast of decay and newness being born from dilapidated sections. "New sounds like before?"

"Revue of up-and-coming talents from every plane known to man and off-planer."

Kate couldn't help but grin. It was like the nanobots had rearranged the muscles on her face. "Wow. So I guess you've been busy since the last time I saw you,"

"That was a year ago," Alicia reminded her.

"A year ago?"

"Yep."

"Seriously?"

Alicia nodded. "Time flies, sis, and it just flew right by you."

"So, should I say that 'Chevroness' dumped Ambush to strike out on her own?

Alicia spat air from her lips. "When we're up for a Grammy? You wish. We're just taking a little break. The tour was rough; you ever been to Shenijen? Laws of physics are bass-ackwards crazy there; makes our music sound way different. And that's not the only world like that, you know. By the end of our tour, my migraines were starting to have baby migraines."

"And now you're going to start a club for amateurs?" Kate laughed. "I fail to see how that's going to relax you, but whatever floats your boat, sis. Good luck with that."

Alicia gave an abrupt and infectious start when the powerful green light suddenly appeared in the corner of Kate's eye, and then moved across her field of vision. Kate winced reflexively, and her eyes trailed the beam to a device held by Mukai, who had appeared almost out of nowhere.

"God, Mukai, you almost made me piss my uniform!" Kate exclaimed, and then exhaled in relief. Her biocomp registered the beam as a combination of magnetic waves used in brain scans, and then suggested a mild sedative injection, which she refused. "Wait," she glanced back to the rows of booths, a nearly impossible notion appearing in her mind, and just as soon dismissed. "You can't possibly be finished checking all those booths already."

"I am." Mukai gave a very casual nod, as if such a feat were nothing. She then pointed her device towards Alicia, who flinched slightly as the green light passed over her.

Kate had been about to protest; technology-wise, Gaea was a slightly backwater world, but then her biocomp brought information of the League's new labor exchange program, which Garrett's data said that Mukai was a part of, to mind. And even in her home dimension, she had been damn good at her work.

A shrill chirp came from Mukai's device.

"A match in brainwave/OnBoard algorithms," Mukai explained before Kate could ask. Her friend cast her liquid black-eyed gaze directly towards Alicia. "She is who we are looking for."

"Wh…Who-?" Kate sputtered at the news, which had not quite registered in her mind, but slowly, like a slow data feed from her biocomp, began to clarify in frightening detail. "I mean what the-? You can't be … Her? No, no, no!"

Her biocomp flashed several accelerated heart rate warnings as she yanked the device from Mukai. Her suit was capable of performing brain scans of its own, but she had to prove that the programming of Mukai's scanner was faulty. There was no way her sister could be their target. From her hand, tendrils of nanofibers slithered into the device's transmitter, which fed the readouts into her field of vision. The uniform adapted to the device's programming and then released a diode which protruded from her shoulder and scanned Alicia, who stood like a deer frozen in headlights. As it had on the device, it came back positive.

Suddenly cold all over, Kate backed away from her sister, her steps halting and trembling as Mukai placidly watched on. How the hell could her own sister be MAGI? This seemed a nightmare of multiple levels of wrongness. Her voice was a pained groan when she finally spoke. "No. God, Aly … why?"

Her expression as immutable as Mukai's, Alicia stepped forward. She opened her mouth to speak, but whether it was to deny or explain, Kate never knew, as several things happened at once.

The air grew colder, and Kate knew that it was not because of her emotional state, especially when a buzz and priority message from her biocomp issued the alarm.

*WARNING. MULTIPLE SUBSPACE RIFTS DETECTED.*

Kate tensed inwardly, but loosened her body to a combat-ready stance. She felt the weapons forming in her uniform's mass reservoirs, but refrained from ejecting them.

How many? She sent the thought to her biocomp.

*NINE RIFTS TOTAL. LEAGUE I.F.F. SIGNAL CONFIRMED IN FIVE: FOUR, FIVE, SIX, SEVEN, AND EIGHT O'CLOCK FROM CURRENT POSITION. SIGNAL NEGATIVE AT ELEVEN, TWELVE, TWELVE-THIRTY, AND ONE O'CLOCK FROM CURRENT POSITION.*

The air – no, it was space itself – rippled from behind and in front of her, and behind where Alicia stood. From the rifts in back, a small force of C-class enforcers appeared, armed with magnetic rail rifles, and shielded with thick spidersilk vests and black helmets. A clear spark of consternation flashed through Kate in the midst of her conflicting emotions. Having backup unrequested, and with this much overkill in weaponry, showed a complete lack of faith on the director's part. Garrett well knew that an A-class was more than capable of bringing in one girl, her sister or not.

But then, the beings who stepped out of the rifts behind Alicia snuck doubt into her confidence. Their silver cloaks confused her for a moment, but as their forms clarified once they emerged from the event horizon, they were quite different: off-planers all, each from a different dimension. One was female, green-skinned, and with hair that looked like electrical wiring. Another was ethereal and fairy-like, with wings that folded over her willowy features, honey blonde hair, and cloak, like sparkling veins running through its diaphanous material. Another was wide-bodied and brutish, like a werewolf and

gorilla mixed together, while another had a face so heavily tattooed, it was impossible to determine anything at all about him.

"Hey now… no need to get hostile, sis," Alicia said, making a gentle placating gesture –one the enforcers responded to with the harmonized crescendo of their weapons' accelerators powering up.

"Stand down!" Kate ordered, giving a stern gesture to the enforcers. But they held their positions. Kate gaped, half in irritation, half in fear.

"They won't listen to you," the green-skinned one said in an unexpectedly high voice. "Their orders come from the director himself."

"W- what do you want?" Kate demanded, the fingers on her gloved hand extending into claws, and retracting in response to her confusion. She pointed at Alicia and the assembled MAGI. Were they MAGI? There was no way to know, but her gut instinct practically screamed an affirmative. "You've never appeared anywhere en masse."

"Haven't we?" Green Skin said, almost amused.

"What's going on, then?" Kate demanded. "Why is my sister one of you?"

"This isn't what you think," Alicia said in a calm, but stern voice. "In fact, nothing you see here is."

"Not your job, not the League… Your whole life after Cybersoft has been practically a lie," Green Skin said.

"How do you know about Cybersoft?" Kate said, ignoring the foolishness of that question. It didn't take a hacker to find out her job history, after all. "Aly, please! Why are you with them?"

"I've always been with them," Alicia replied matter-of-factly. "Katie, there's so much we want to tell you, but … now's not the time, you know? And they know too much already."

"'They'? Who are 'they'?" Alicia said, and swallowed hard against a dry throat.

"The League," Green Skin replied.

"We can tell you more later," Alicia said.

"Enough talk," Mukai said, boldly stepping towards Alicia, as if the assembled MAGI were invisible to her. She reached into the obi sash of her uniform and removed a pistol.

"Mukai, what the hell are you doing?" Kate said through gritted teeth. Her biocomp made a series of shrill medical warnings which she effectively silenced with a thought.

"She must be arrested, or terminated," Mukai said.

"Are you out of your freaking mind?" Kate exclaimed. "That's my sister; there's no way in hell you're going to kill her!"

"We have our orders, friend Kate."

"No. My orders," Kate said with finality. "With all due respect, Mukai, you're not an enforcer; you're a …" she paused as her translation matrix sought the correct word in Glossiu, "… a 'techie.'" She shifted her gaze back to her sister. "Aly. Come with me to League HQ; we can talk about this. If worse comes to worst, my lawyers can defend -"

Mukai's gunshot echoed in the restaurant, and in Kate's mind, it became the only sound, fragmented by the image of horror that broke her: Alicia's lifeless body falling to the ground, a ribbon of blood from her wounded skull, the only image in her mind's eye.

She did not know who screamed: herself, Mukai, the enforcers, the MAGI, or even the customers as they fled in panicked terror, but in the corner of her mind that could analyze, she knew the machine had taken over. In the end, when the blood and various off-plane ichors painted the still-repairing stage and floor, and the molecule-thin blades retracted into her uniform, Kate knew that the present scream belonged to her. Exploding grief and anguish and guilt echoed into a crescendo of pain…

…And then vanished.

The world was then replaced with the oddest – and most unpleasant – mix of sensations: a combination of severe vertigo and planar dysphoria: the result of shifting dimensions too rapidly. She retched into a prepared bucket, as a voice spoke soothing words to her. She felt something like a hand upon her back, holding her thick black hair away from her face as the contents of her stomach emptied in the backwash from the horrifying shock to her senses.

"There, there," the voice said. Through her sickness, Kate realized by tone and accent that it was Dr. Galt who spoke to her, and that it was one of his pseudopods upon her back instead of his tiny, ugly hands. "The sickness is commonplace for what you went through. You passed, you know."

"Passed..?" Kate quavered in the midst of coughing after the nausea passed. She spat out the acidic remnants of bile and gingerly wiped her mouth with the back of her hand. A glass of water was presented to her, and she accepted it, taking small sips as to not set off the nausea again. "W … what happened? Where's Aly? Mukai? I was at Pink's … I think. I saw the MAGI …"

"You were sedated, and hooked to a VRSense network," the doctor said, letting go of Kate's hair as she struggled to sit up in the chair. "The mission, the betrayal: all of it was a simulation. All part of your psych exam."

The totality of everything that had happened, and the scope of the doctor's words at last registered. But strangely, she made little reaction to it. Her body still seemed to not accept it.

"So none of it happened?" Kate swallowed another sip of water that had suddenly gone tepid in her mouth. How'd you sedate…?" She froze with cold realization. "The tea!"

"I … ah … apologize for the deception, Lieutenant Barnes." His tone was shaky and mawkish and he began to stutter. It became clear to Kate that the Doctor was beginning to feel the full brunt of her emotions. "B-but we had to give you a s-s-simulation that you would accept … as completely real."

"You didn't have to do it the last time," Kate's voice came out distant and hollow as her initial shock receded and slowly gave way to burning rage. This was nothing else but a violation. The little four-armed creature had put her under and stuck her brain in a computer, running it through scenarios like a rat in a maze. Screw the purpose; this was akin to rape.

"W-we have t-to randomize the test for each p-p-participant, so that the r-results cannot be manip-manipulated by familiarity," the doctor attempted to explain in a voice that cracked like a squeaky wagon wheel. But by now, Kate was beyond either listening or caring. Her eyes downcast, she forced back the tirade that was building in her throat. "And you have to appreciate t-the ultimate harmlessness of ... of the whole ordeal."

Something inside Kate snapped.

"Harmless?" She shot out of the seat, and in one fluid bionic movement, slid forward and grabbed the doctor by the collar of his bodysuit. She glared death into the beady green eyes that were set into the doctor's profusely sweating face. Baring her teeth as her biocomp rippled with weapons options and warnings, she noticed in her peripheral vision the dark patch that had begun to grow in the lower part of the doctor's uniform, as well as a sudden acrid acetone stench that grew in the air.

"You made me watch while one of my best friends killed my sister, you misshapen little kridball!" She stepped forward, and the doctor staggered backwards, his sweat exuding the pungent smell of acetone ever more. "Well, if you think that was harmless, then maybe you'll think this –" She narrowed the width of the heel on her foot padding, and stomped hard on a supporting pseudopod, "– is harmless!"

The doctor howled in pain. A black ichor from his wounded appendage stained the carpet as he collapsed against the wall behind him, exploding a string of expletives in his guttural native tongue. The biocomp offered a translation, and Kate declined as she stormed out of the lab. Several league techies gave her a wide berth when the exit door slid open.

The full force of her emotions came out much later, after the tedium of the calibration tests, when Kate at long last removed the uniform. It hurt like hell as it peeled off of her body in the shower stall, breaking some of her skin. Tiny rivulets of blood washed down the drain as she collapsed to the floor and huddled into a ball, her legs drawn against herself under the warm water's constant assault upon her raw skin. Truly alone now, away from the prying eyes of cameras and her uniform's biocomp, she cried.

Kate's true shame burned like a wound much deeper within. If it were weakness the doctor had been searching for, then he had indeed found it.

Through all the implants and the near-invulnerable protection the uniform offered, an enforcer, the League's most elite defense force, was still a frail being in mind. Perhaps this was the reason that not a tear that Kate shed was from the pain that the nanomaterial had left behind.

THE END

# RAGE

Available online at:

Amazon.com
Barnesandnoble.com
iTunes
Scribd
Oyster
Smashwords
and others

Karen Bechard, UN Agent, thought the flight from the US to Europe was going to be routine. It was in mid flight where everything turned ugly. A man hyped on some highly addictive drug goes zombie flesh eating berserk. People die, people get hurt, and then no one to fly the plane. What is an agent to do? And, that was the easy part of the day, of which was turning out to be a Four Horsemen trampling humanity scenario and Karen had to be on her A-game.

EXTRA ES SOLAR
NO DOMINION

J. Ryan Malone 2010
irmalone.deviantart.com

bovistock.deviantart.com

EXTRA ES SOLAR
ariel-x.deviantart.com
2011

EXTRASOLAR NOMAD LEGACY
one 2012
ariel-x.deviantart.com

jrmalone.deviantart.com

joakimolofsson.deviantart.com

bovistock.deviantart.com

# EXTRA SOLAR

WILHEARD. GLADWIN. BELT

SEPTEMBER 5TH 1837

ariel-x.deviantart.com

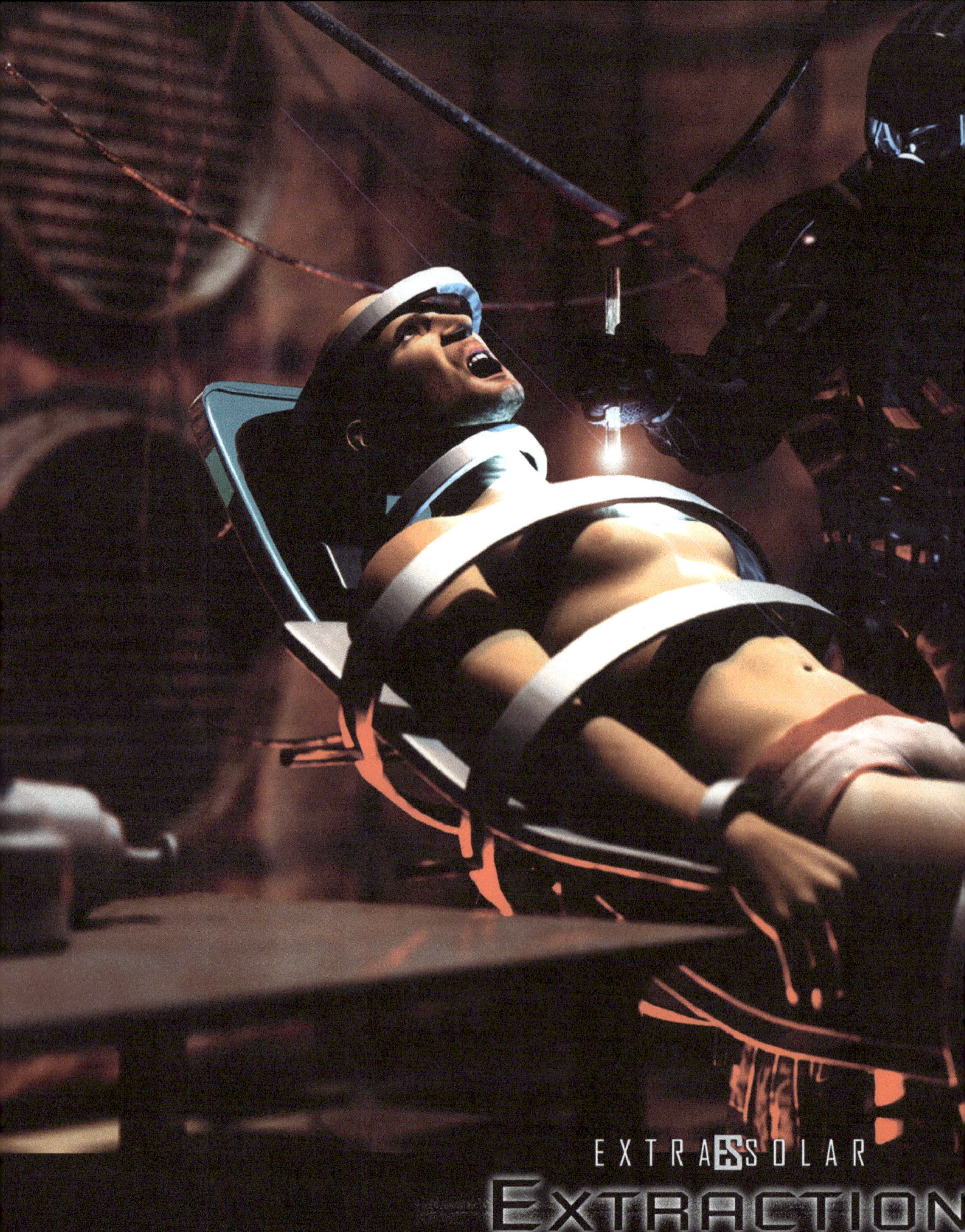

EXTRA SOLAR
EXTRACTION

J. Ryan Malone 2010
jrmalone.deviantart.com

The Birth of Karen

bovistock.deviantart.com

HOME TO ALL THINGS BLACK SCIENCEFICTION
BLACKSCIENCEFICTION SOCIETY
BOOKS, COMICS, MOVIES, EVENTS, GAMES, TOYS, MAGAZINES, RADIO SHOWS, FORUMS, GROUPS & MORE...
MEMBERSHIP IS FREE!
www.BlackScienceFictionSociety.com

# GEMP

## J Carrell Jones

. . . continued from part 1

## Chapter 5

It was 1:39 am and Kelly couldn't sleep. Neither Steve nor Kelly felt like talking when they got back to their room. They checked in on Oscar, who was fast asleep and dreaming. Both washed up, ate a quick meal from the pantry and went to bed. Then, she just woke up. "Steve, you awake?"

Steve snoozed softly while drooling on his pillow. "Steve! You awake?"

Steve rolled over. "Not yet. Why?"

"Because I can't sleep."

With his back still facing Kelly he said, "And you want me to share in your insomnia?"

"No, well . . . no . . . yes. I do."

Steve yawned and rolled back over.

"What are we going to do about the Gemps?"

"Which ones?"

"Both."

Steve took a deep breath. This was going to be a long night. "Kelly. Government property, remember? I don't like it either, but we both signed the dotted line. Uncle Sam is paying for our retirement."

"But they are alive. They think for God's sake. They think and have emotions."

"I know, but I don't think Ken meant Mos' group would be killed."

"That's not how I heard him."

"Ken said the wild Gemps are an evolutionary dead-end. He said no such thing about Mos."

"Steve, that's the point. One group gets killed . . ."

"Maybe. We don't know the big picture."

"Okay, one group may get killed and the other something. What's the something? Research? Medical experiments. Zoos?"

Steve thought a moment. 'Zoos.' Very illogical, but who blames the Government for thinking logically? "I think there really is something

bigger going on here, but I'm too sleepy to talk about it. Just a few more hours . . . of . . ." and he started snoozing again.

Kelly watched him. "Should she be mad? She gave the thought a few minutes to germinate. Yes, she should be. He fell asleep while they were talking. She thought she should give him the silent treatment in the morning and have him wonder what he did wrong all day. Men! Never quite understanding what is important.

***

Steve woke up with a start. He dreamt he was talking to Kelly in the middle of the night and fell asleep while they were talking. He shook the fogginess from his head. It was just a dream he eventually convinced himself. Steve stretched, yawned, and got up. It was 5:30 am. The morning briefing would be in another four hours, so he decided a quick wash up and a trip to the base gym, before breakfast, would be a good thing. When he got there Kelly was already working a Stairmaster. He walked up to an empty station next to Kelly. He climbed up and leaned in to say 'morning'.

Kelly saw when Steve walked in. He spotted her, smiled, and stopped at a station next to her's. She pretended not to notice him. When he leaned in to say 'hi' she looked away casually.

Steve tapped Kelly on the shoulder.

She turned, said, "Morning," then looked away again.

Realization hit Steve. It wasn't a dream. He'd known Kelly long enough to know that she'd find an in to tell him what he did wrong. He sighed deeply, placed the earplugs attached to his smartphone into his ears and started exercising.

***

Oscar had left that morning early. He had an agenda. His destination would be the Gemps. It was worked out. He'd seen it on Television many times. He watched some of the male soldiers use it on the female soldiers and civilians. PFC Haynes greeted

him at one of the secured entrance into the Gemp camp. This entrance was made especially for him.

"Greetings Oscar," the young private said.

Oscar gave him a toothy smile.

Haynes checked today's activity. "Oscar, I don't see an authorized schedule outing today."

Oscar signed, "Special assignment. Very important."

The young man eyed Oscar, "Is that so? Is this something I can mention to Dr. Launse when I see him?"

Oscar hooted a few times. He worked his mouth as if he were talking to Haynes. Then he produced an L-Ration card. Steve had about three years' worth stockpiled in his office. It was meant to be used on the mainland.

Haynes smiled. The last L-Ration card Oscar gave him had about three hundred dollars on it. The card disappeared somewhere in the Private's pants pocket. He simply said, "I'll let Reynolds know you are out. Treat him well, too."

Oscar raised the fingertips of an open right hand to his lips and he gently moved them away as if blowing a kiss. In a way, it was just that. This was more than a thank you if it worked.

The path to the village was long. It usually took about 30 minutes if he wasn't in a hurry. When he emerged from the hidden passageway the Sun had just started to rise. It was another fifteen minutes' walk to the village. Oscar had decided he would approach Hela, first. Whenever he was in the village she seemed to pay more attention to him. She was also the most attentive student he had whenever he taught them new signs. As a backup plan, he brought chocolate. He quickened his pace and made it to the village fringe in less than five minutes. He slowly approached Hela's shelter. Stepping around to the entrance he quickly peered inside. Empty.

She had to be down by the river.

He causally walked the short distance and found her with Feme. Both had found fruit and were washing it for an early meal.

Feme heard the break of twigs first. She turned

thinking it would be Tutu and one of the other Gemps. She tapped Hela when she saw the Elder. Both giggled as the Elder slowly made his way toward them.

Oscar signed, "Children. Morning. Good to see pretty Hela and Feme."

Both signed and said, "Elder. We are surprised to see you."

Oscar replied, "Really? God sent me to check on his children."

Hela and Feme excitedly ran up to Oscar.

Feme signed, "Elder, it was frightening last night. The sky flashed bright many times followed by loud boom sounds."

Hela followed with, "And Mos ran into the village. He said God made the light and sound."

Oscar signed, "And Tutu did not believe him."

"Elder!" Hela said. "How did you know?"

"God sent me to check on his children."

The two Gemps were excited. They giggled. "Elder, you must tell the village."

Oscar signed, "Stop. Not yet. Elder wants to talk to both of you."

The two settled down. "Yes, Elder?" Feme said.

"The Elder favors you two."

They blushed.

"You have a special place in Elder's heart."

They giggled and leaned into one another.

"Elder would like to show how much he favors Hela and Feme. Will you let me show you?"

Hela asked, "How, Elder?"

"May I touch you in a special place?"

They blinked.

"Come. Let's not wake the others yet. Let us go into Hela's shelter. Just the three of us."

They hesitated. "Are you going to hurt us like Tutu and Gitu?"

Oscar shook his head. "Elder favors the two and will be kind. He has a treat." Two pieces of chocolate appeared in his hand. He finger spelt, "C H O C O L A T E." He motioned for them to eat it.

Each Gemp took a piece. They sniffed and lightly licked at the heart shaped milk chocolate pieces. Each piece was as big as a thumb.

Hela pronounced, "Choke O Late?"

Oscar bit into air and signed, "Bite. Surprise inside."

Feme bit first. Her eyes widened and she savored the sweet innards. She sucked in the gooey cherry gel leaving the heart empty.

Hela watched Feme. It must be good she thought and took a bite. The cherry flavor mixed in with the milk chocolate coating burst into her mouth. She look at Oscar, who was staring intently at her, and wanted another. The deliciously gooey filling coated her teeth and tongue and made her salivate.

Both signed, "More, please. May I have another?"

Oscar smiled, "Elder wants to favor Feme and Hela. We go to Hela shelter. Oscar has appetite for pretty Feme and Hela."

The two blushed and still licking their lips walked, without a word back into the village. Everyone was still asleep, which was good. They walked passed Kiri's shelter and heard what sounded like Mos' voice. They knew what he was doing. He favored Kiri. Now Elder was going to favor them and both became excited. The Elder was going to give them more chocolate. As they reached Hela's Shelter, both Gemps looked at each other and nodded. Elder knew God and he had chocolate, too.

***

Steve set his tray of fruit, toast, and Greek yogurt next to Kelly.

She was eating a bagel. A half empty cup of coffee was in her hands. She stared blankly at a wall behind Steve.

"Kelly, I'm sorry. I was so tired, I . . ."

". . . asleep while we were talking."

"It was one something in the morning."

"1:39 am . . . and you fell asleep. This was important."

Steve knew it was fruitless to argue. He would never win this battle. It wasn't worth the mental ammo. "Kelly, I am sorry. Really. I'm awake now."

"The moment passed," She said.

Steve sighed.

The two ate in silence.

A few minutes later Grenier walked into the

cafeteria, spotted Steve and Kelly. He hurried over to the two with an alarmed look on his face.

Kelly noticed Grenier first. She reached over and touched Steve on the sleeve, her anger forgotten. "Steve," she said.

Grenier sat down. "Steve, we have a situation."

"The Gemps?!?"

"Worse, Oscar."

Kelly said, "Oh my God. Is he okay?"

"You two need to see this." He got up and left.

Kelly got up first with Steve very close.

All three walked into Briefing Room Three. It was the only room with a large 110 inch flat screen. Rogers, the morning shift supervisor, sat at one end of the conference table. He had a media control tablet in front of him. Colonel Codper, scowling, sat at the other.

Kelly and Steve sat in the middle on one side, Grenier the other.

Kelly, still worried, said, "Is Oscar alright?"

Codper spoke, "More than alright, Ma'am. Damn near perfect."

She gave him an inquisitive look.

Grenier nodded at Rogers.

Rogers tapped on the tablet a few times. The lights dimmed and the flat screen came on. He moved out of the way so that the others could see the entire screen. "At 0545 PFC Haynes allowed Oscar unauthorized entry into Gemp Village One." He narrated.

The screen showed several images of Oscar moving through the passageway. The first few moments he was moving at a regular pace, then suddenly he picked up his pace and practically started running. Clearly he was on a mission and agenda of his own making.

Rogers tapped at the tablet.

The video changed to Oscar with Hela and Feme by the riverbank.

Codper asked, "What is he doing?"

Steve watched with dread. He followed the conversation. "Oscar is tempting the two."

"Tempting," Codper began, "Tempting them for . . ." his voice trailed off.

Everyone watched as the camera showed Hela and Feme each eat a heart shaped chocolate filled with something. Kelly identified with their reactions. Then the three headed into the village. The video switched to show the three entering Hela's shelter. The screen went dark.

The room remained silent for a moment.

Codper said, "Did that little chimp of yours do what I think he did? Did he fornicate with the Gemps?"

Steve turned to face the Colonel. "I can't believe Oscar would . . . shit."

Codper said, "Son, that little bastard monkey of yours is out of control."

"I take offense to that, Colonel. Oscar is not out of control and he is not a bastard."

Codper stood up, outraged, yelled while pointing to the screen, "What did we just watch?"

"Oscar doing what . . ."

Codper yelled, ". . . he's not supposed to be doing that."

"Colonel, he's still an animal with urges. He's . . ."

". . . fucking those beast!"

Kelly had a distressed look on her face. She thought for a moment and said, "Isn't this exactly what we wanted?"

Everyone tuned to face her.

Grenier said, "Kelly, what do you mean?"

"Think about it. Oscar is the only one on this base who either doesn't have a partner or can't go to the mainland for outlet. He's stuck on this island with humans and Gemps."

Steve sucked in his lips, "She's right. I hadn't thought about that. Damn!"

Codper said, "So we let this chimp of yours fornicate with the Gemps?"

Grenier said, "Yes."

Codper turned, "What?!?"

Grenier turned to Steve. "Steve, what have men in power done over the ages?"

"Most have abused it. History is full of examples."

Grenier said, "What about religion?"

Steve said, "Some of the worse examples of abuse."

Codper sat down, "Outrageous. No man of God would ever abuse his position."

Steve replied, "Colonel, the bible is full of

examples. Maybe it's how you look at it?"

"There is only one way to read the Bible, son. It is . . ."

"Haman."

"Pardon?"

"Haman, Colonel. He was the vizier of King Ahasuerus. If it wasn't for Esther the entire Hebrew nation would have been wiped out. And there's Herod. Judas. Pilate. Simon. All men of power. The bible shows that eventually those who abuse power fail and fall."

Codper nodded. He had just finished reading Matthew 26 and 27. "Okay, son. I get it, but that still doesn't excuse the fact of your little monkey fornicating."

Grenier said, "Colonel, you're missing the point. This is a fluid experiment. Nothing is set in stone here."

The Colonel was about to call Grenier son but remembered last night. "What do you suggest we do?"

"Steve, I think this is the best thing to happen. Think of it. Oscar is showing us the development of corruption of power. He's learned to work the system and is now using it to his advantage. We got two experiments going here."

Steve took a deep breath. Grenier was right. He looked over to Kelly.

She smiled. Even though it was gross on some levels she also saw it as very sweet. Oscar having a girlfriend or two.

"Okay, we let Oscar continue, but I think we should punish him in some way."

Codper said, "I'm not likely this one bit. This project seems to me is getting out of hand."

"In what way?" Grenier said.

Codper remained silent. Civilians he thought. Non believing heathens.

"Colonel, we are gathering information."

"At the tax payers' expense." Codper spat.

Grenier retorted, "And the Military cost what each year?"

Codper stood up.

Grenier stood up and leaned forward. "The project is not in jeopardy, Colonel."

The two men stared at one another for an undetermined amount of seconds.

Codper blinked again. "A standing army is vital in a world full of evil."

Grenier answered, "Especially when we are the cause of such evil. Colonel, look, we walked into this project knowing that all sorts of unknowns were going to pop up. This is one. It won't be the last."

Codper sat down. "I'm adding this to my report to the Chairman."

Grenier nodded, "And I'm adding this to my report to the President and Joint Chief of Staff."

Steve and Kelly held their breath. Codper and Grenier clashed before, but not like this.

Rogers coughed. "Sirs, briefing is in another 30 minutes."

Codper said, "Understood."

Grenier looked at his watch. "My suggestion is to not mention this incident while Oscar is here. I'd like him to think he got away with his adventure."

Codper said, "And that will accomplish what?"

"Let him continue. We can observe him and the Gemps. That is the reason we made him 'The Elder.'"

Steve nodded, "True, but for him to think he got away is . . ."

". . . is good. Let's work this out. How far will he go? Will the other male Gemps challenge him? Will God's might be enough for Oscar to keep his position? We just had another can of worms opened. Plump and juicy. I say we let it ride."

Kelly nodded. "I agree, but for different reasons."

All the males turned to her.

Grenier asked, "Such?"

"It's not that I like the idea of Oscar turning into an alpha dominating misogynistic male, but that Hela and Feme are in a position of power. You've read the book, 'The Power of the Pussy', right?"

She got blank stirs.

Men she thought. Bright as door knobs sometimes. "Look, Oscar wants something. Apparently, he went to great lengths to get it. I used to think men had it so easy in enticing women, but I'm seeing it differently now. First, Oscar had to be in a position that got him noticed. Next, he had to dream up his plan. He needed the means and materials. Then he had to execute it. If anything, I'd wonder how one, Oscar got the chocolate and second, got PFC Hayes to allow him to leave unauthorized. Guys, Oscar has been working the system for years to his advantage. Seems to me, we wanted to make Gemps human. Instead, we made a chimpanzee human as well. But anyway, as I was saying, Hela and Feme are in a position to work the system themselves. They are getting chocolate in exchange for Oscar's needs."

"Fornicating!" Codper spat.

Kelly continued, "The Gemps have been sexually active for about a year now and . . ."

Codper said, "Disgusting little beasts."

Kelly scowled, "Disgusting? Colonel, are you living in the Dark Ages?"

"I just don't like the thought of all this."

Kelly eyed him for a few seconds, but decided to not push. Clearly the Colonel had issues but this was not the time to air his dirty laundry. She said, "Oscar should continue and, of course, we should watch him."

Grenier nodded, "Colonel, I know there has been a breach in discipline and protocol in one or more instance, but I strongly urge you to allow it to continue. Talk to PFC Hayes, if you must, but don't spook him. Punish him later, but not now."

"Don't tell me how to discipline my men . . ."

Grenier raised his voice a little louder than he had wanted, "God damn it Colonel! No one is stepping on your dick . . ." He blushed, turned to Kelly, "Sorry," turned back to Codper, "This is an opportunity of getting good data. This, as odd as it seems, is the reason for spending all this money. The emergence of Human behavior, good, bad, or indifferent, by non-humans." He was red in the cheeks. If he could have the Colonel replaced he would, but the Chairman favored him. Fuck! Grenier thought.

Codper stared at Grenier a long time. He'd let the little monkey continue. He'll have the duty sergeant watch Haynes closer. He'll give Garner what he wanted, but he would recommend to the Chairman the project be terminated, and the Gemps destroyed. He'd see Grenier pushing the unemployment line and it would be good. "Alright. We'll let the little chimp continue . . . for now."

"Thank you," Grenier said.

***

Oscar used up his quota of chocolate for the month early. He had another week of waiting and that was much too long. Feme and Hela wanted chocolate and he wanted them.

Sergeant Farmers was behind his desk. He knew Oscar wanted something the moment the little chimp rounded the corner. "Oscar!" He signed, "Hello."

Oscar jumped up onto a chair next to Farmers' desk. He signed, "Chocolate. You have?"

Farmers said, "Of course, Oscar." He smiled. "I always reserve extra for you, but . . ."

Oscar produced a L-Ration card.

Farmers leaned back into his chair. "How many boxes?"

Oscar remembered the first time he tried this. He asked for one box. When he came back for another Farmers said he needed another L-Ration card. Oscar was so furious he thought about ripping the man's arm off and beating him with it. He learned over the years. He signed, "Give me two now. Two next week. Two week after that."

Farmers nodded. The chimp learned some bargaining over the years. Besides, he liked Oscar. Everyone did. Oscar had a cache of L-Rations and that made it even better. "Done. Flavor filling, nuts, or solid?"

"One box flavor. One box mixed, please."

A few minutes later Oscar had his two boxes. He hurried to his room to drop the boxes off before this morning's briefing. He'd ration them out to Feme and Hela over a week time. Today he'd get his outing schedule.

## Chapter 6

After the morning briefing Codper went to his room. "Heathens!" He spat. The bottle of whiskey sat next to his computer keyboard on his desk. He reached for the cup next to it and blew inside. He poured a healthy dose of booze and swallowed half of it in one gulp. Then filled the cup again and sipped this time. He sat back in his chair and stared at a blank monitor. His bible was within reach and when he touched it he immediately felt at ease in a way adult beverage would never make him feel. He turned to Deuteronomy.

*"Neither shalt thou bring an abomination into thine house, lest thou be a cursed thing like it: but thou shalt utterly detest it, and thou shalt utterly abhor it; for it is a cursed thing." – Deuteronomy 7:26*

He finished the cup and poured another.

***

Oscar had a feeling that something changed. Everyone in the room avoided looking at him directly. It took him years to understand that when humans look you in the eye it is not a challenge. He sat in between Kelly and Steve. Kelly smiled down at him and gave him a hug. She almost never did that. Steve made idle talk. He asked about his evening and did he read anything special. He asked if he wanted to talk about something. Oscar caught a frown from Grenier. It disappeared when he saw Oscar staring and he smiled. The Colonel was in a foul mood. He was almost always in a foul mode. Recently, he started smelling like naughty-water. This morning was no exception. His face was scrunched up during the entire meeting, but that meant little to Oscar. He was thinking of Hela and Feme and this morning. He started to become excited again, but quickly thought of something else. Like TV and video games, but both the Gemps sure felt good. Everyone agreed he should visit the Village daily, which of course he didn't mind. That was the best news. Ever.

***

*"But when the righteous turneth away from his righteousness, and committeth iniquity, and doeth according to all the abominations that the wicked man doeth, shall he live? All his righteousness that he hath done shall not be mentioned: in his trespass that he hath trespassed, and in his sin that he hath sinned, in*

*them shall he die." – Ezekiel 18:24*

He poured another.
***

Oscar hurried to his room. He found a small pouch he could use to carry some chocolate. He put in some chewy filling ones and a few with nut centers. He hoped the first box would last a couple of days.

***

*"Watch and pray, that ye enter not into temptation: the spirit indeed is willing, but the flesh is weak." – Matthew 26:41*

He poured another.
***

Oscar emerged from the passageway and casually walked to the village. He made his way to the river bank and entered from there. Most of the Gemps were sitting around grooming one another. Hela and Feme sat near Mos and Kiri, talking. Mos had picked figs earlier and now shared them. Kiri had several pomegranates between her legs. She handed one to Mos and another to Hela and Feme. They looked up and saw Oscar.

***

*"There hath no temptation taken you but such as is common to man: but God is faithful, who will not suffer you to be tempted above that ye are able; but will with the temptation also make a way to escape, that ye may be able to bear it." – Corinthians 10:13*

His hand slipped and some whiskey missed the cup.

***

Steve, Kelly, and Grenier sat in the observation room. Two of the large monitors were focused on Mos and those around him. Oscar came into view and sat in the center. Hela and Feme blushed and acted shy. Mos signed, "Elder, Mos has questions about God."

Oscar replied, "My child, ask."

Grenier leaned back in his chair, "If only I had popcorn."

Steve shot Grenier a quick glance, "Ken, this is serious. What are we doing?"

Grenier leaned forward to get a better look at Steve, "We just doubled down. All that happens now is just profit. Nothing lost everything gained." He leaned back again.

Kelly asked, "How so?"

Grenier answered, "Oscar. Ironically, he's our human link.

***

*"I will make mine arrows drunk with blood, and my sword shall devour flesh; and that with the blood of the slain and of the captives, from the beginning of revenges upon the enemy." – Deuteronomy 32:42*

He misjudged the distance and grabbed air. The second attempt he grabbed cup and drank.

***

Oscar signed, "God is like us, but taller. He is smart. Knows a lot about many things. He watches us. He takes care of us." Then Oscar remembered the key item he had to slip in. He took his right index finger, lifted up his left elbow to his chest level and struck it lightly and quick with the index finger. He finger spelled "PUNISH".

The three imitated Oscar.

Mos pronounced it, "Poo-nish."

Oscar shook his head and signed "Sounds like RUN." He hooked a right hand index finger "L" around his left hand index "L" thumb. Both hands had the index fingers parallel to the ground with the thumbs up. He quickly thrusted both hands away from him quickly.

Mos nodded, said,"Pun-ish."

Oscar gave him a toothy smile.

The others pronounced the word.

Oscar clapped.

Feme asked, "What does this word mean?"

***

*"And after all that is come upon us for our evil deeds, and for our great trespass, seeing that thou our God hast punished us less than our iniquities deserve, and hast given us such deliverance as this;*

*Should we again break thy commandments, and join in affinity with the people of these abominations? wouldest not thou be angry with us till thou hadst consumed us, so that there should be no remnant nor escaping?" – Ezra 9:13 - 14*

He stopped drinking. He was satisfied with his heavy buzz.

***

Oscar signed, "God would take away all that is good. No food. No shelter. No clothing." He looked at Hela and Feme. "No chocolate."

Mos and Kiri gave Oscar a curious look.

Hela and Feme frowned and tears welled up in their eyes.

Oscar continued, "Listen to God. Follow his ways and his teachings through me and you shall be rewarded."

Mos said, "I believe in God." He pointed to himself, pointed to his forehead and clasped his hands together in front of him. He finger spelt "IN" and finished with a right hand index finger to the sky and bringing the hand down open palm fingers slightly spread palm facing left to chest level.

***

*"For the stars of heaven and the constellations thereof shall not give their light: the sun shall be darkened in his going forth, and the moon shall not cause her light to shine.*

*And I will punish the world for their evil, and the wicked for their iniquity; and I will cause the arrogancy of the proud to cease, and will lay low the haughtiness of the terrible.*

*I will make a man more precious than fine gold; even a man than the golden wedge of Ophir." – Isaiah 13:10-12*

He turned on his computer and waited precious seconds for the welcome screen to appear. His email program started immediately. Within a minute he saw a message from the Chairman embedded in a stream of other messages. He clicked on the Chairman's and read. It was a simple email. It read,

My good Colonel,

I agree, the situation is dire and deserves further congressional oversight. The President, the Joint Chief of Staff, DARPA and the NBAC are behind this project - fully. This is not a battle that can be fought by committee.

*"Then I proclaimed a fast there, at the river of Ahava, that we might afflict ourselves before our God, to seek of him a right way for us, and for our little ones, and for all our substance.*

*For I was ashamed to require of the king a band of soldiers and horsemen to help us against the enemy in the way: because we had spoken unto the king, saying, The hand of our God is upon all them for good that seek him; but his power and his wrath is against all them that forsake him.*

*So we fasted and besought our God for this: and he was intreated of us." – Ezra 8:21-23*

May you find the strength, my friend, to do what is right in your heart.

With all sincerity,

B.

His heavy buzz faded quickly. He was on his own now. A pity.

***

Tutu walked over to Oscar. He said and signed, "Tutu, not believe. No proof."

Oscar stood up. He was still a foot shorter than Tutu, "Do I look like Tutu?"

Tutu frowned, said, "No."

"Do I talk like Tutu?"

"Elder has no voice. Talks with hands."

"Proof God exists. I am different, yet we talk. We . . . "

"Do not see the same thing. I see small Gemp. Hairy. No voice. God is flawed to make Elder funny looking."

Oscar's anger flared up. He thought about hitting Tutu, but decided Steve would be mad and take away his chocolate and TV. He did once before. Oscar screamed and broke anything and everything that was throwable, but Steve stood there and waited. When Oscar finished Steve flew into a chimp-like crazed rage. He chased Oscar around the room screaming, yelling, and throwing things at Oscar. The chimp was terrified. That was the last time Steve had to react extreme. Oscar looked Tutu in the eyes. Steve told him to make sure he doesn't blink first.

Tutu stared back. No one challenged him before like this. The Elder locked gaze and never let up. Tutu felt a growing coldness creep up his back. He was losing his nerve. The Elder won.

Oscar watched as Tutu looked down.

Tutu, feeling disgusted, said, "Tutu no like God or Elder." He looked at Hela and Feme. "Follow me."

Both said, "No."

Tutu gave them a scowl.

Both females stood up and signed, "No."

Tutu, forgetting his encounter with Oscar roared.

The other Gemps around the village scampered from the center. Tutu was mad and someone was going to get hurt.

***

An alarm went off in the Command center. Steve, Kelly, and Grenier were still in the observation room talking. Grenier clicked an intercom button near his seat. "This is Grenier, who triggered that alarm?"

A specialist stood up, 'Sir! Gemps are about to fight."

One of the large monitors showed Tutu puffing out his chest, roaring.

Grenier turned to Steve, said, "Might be a good time to show God? I'm worried that Tutu might hurt Oscar."

"Oh, Steve, Oscar could get hurt." Kelly said.

Steve shook his head, "It's the other way 'round. Oscar is strong enough to rip Tutu to pieces. The Gemps only have two-thirds our strength."

Grenier pressed the Intercom button. "Prepare Mr. Launse for a Day launch. Start to que up clouds and place a rain storm on stand-by." He turned to Steve and released the button. "Agreed?"

Steve nodded, "Agreed."

Grenier pressed the button again, "Mr. Launse is going out in five minutes. Prepare a subterranean launch."

Steve took a deep breath and exhaled. "Kelly, ready? This is it."

She nodded and the two raced out.

Grenier sat back down and wished he had that bag of popcorn. He pulled out his cell phone and called the kitchen. Cookie was on duty. "Cookie, can you bring up a large bag of your home style popcorn to Observation Room one, please?"

A deep voice answered, "Of course, sir. Up in five minutes."

"Perfect! Thanks, I owe you."

Cookie answered, "Tens and twenties, sir."

Both men laughed before Grenier clicked off.

***

The Colonel woke with a start. The alarm sounded. He had been hunched in his chair, in front of the computer. He reached for the phone and dialed the Command center. "What's the alarm about?"

The voice replied, "Gemps, sir. Possible fight. Mr. Launse is about to go out."

Codper grunted, "On the way." He slammed the phone down, contemplated taking another drink but in mid pour changed his mind. He walked into the bathroom and rinsed his mouth in hot water and mouthwash. Damn apes he thought. Abominations, the whole lot.

***

Oscar stepped in front of Tutu. "Both said no," he signed. He knew Steve well enough to know that fighting to protect the Gemps would be okay.

Tutu roared. He swung at Oscar.

Oscar ducked and was glad to have an excuse to hit Tutu. He gave him a two arm slam combo.

Tutu felt Oscar's powerful hands connect. He would not have thought the small chimp could hit so hard. He swung at Oscar again.

Oscar ducked and hit him with another two arm combination. He yelled and hit a third time.

Tutu fell to the ground. He pushed himself away from Oscar and ran to his shelter. He emerged with a bow and arrow.

Oscar stood his ground and snarled.

Tutu took aim.

Hela stepped in front of Oscar and stare hard at Tutu.

Tutu looked up and said, "Hela move. I shoot Elder, not you."

Hela slowly shook her head. "No."

Tutu aimed again.

Feme stepped in front of Hela.

Tutu looked up, growled, "Move, Feme!"

"No." Feme said.

"Then I shoot you first."

Mos and Kiri stepped in front of Feme.

Tutu yelled, "Move! I shoot everyone!"

No one moved.

Tutu roared and ran at the group.

Oscar launched himself at Tutu, chimp screaming the short distance. He avoided Tutu's grab and bite him on the arm. Oscar screamed and started beating Tutu with outstretched arms.

Tutu fell to the ground, curled up into a ball, taking the crazed chimp's powerful arm blows.

Suddenly the ground shook. Fruit from nearby trees dropped to the ground.

Mos fell to the ground, "It is God! God must be angry."

Oscar stopped hitting Tutu. He ran and hide behind Feme and Hela signing, "God mad God mad God mad."

Tutu tried to stand up. He grabbed at the nearest shelter and pulled himself up. Oscar didn't break anything, but he would be feeling the small creature's attack for days. It would be a painful reminder to never piss off a chimp.

Steve heard Oscar's shrill scream over the intercom. Kelly had just finished putting on the last touch of makeup. She rigged him a harness that had a capacitor at the small of his back. It stored enough electricity to drop a raging bull elephant at 20 yards away. With a flick of his wrist, stream of bolt, elephant down. He turned to Staff Sergeant Erwin, who operated the ground shaker and tunnel lift to the surface.

Erwin flipped the switch and massive metal pads underneath the village started vibrating. Randomly a pad would recoil away from the surface and strike hard. Erwin said, "Ready, sir?"

Steve nodded. He was standing in a bowl like platform.

Erwin flipped another switch and two halves of an acrylic cone sealed together to protect him from dirt. Erwin flipped a third switch and Steve started to rise. The surface above him opened up and dirt poured in around him. The platform caught most of it. Fog rolled in and covered the gaping hole Steve was emerging from. Once out in the open the two acrylic halves separated. Dirt spilled in and covered his feet.

The ground stopped shaking and smoke appeared out of nowhere. The bright sky started to turn dark and a hole appeared in the ground. Kiri grabbed Mos' hand and squeezed tightly. All the Gemps watched as a hooded figure appeared from the ground. Mos recognized the figure. He said, "It is God."

Steve stepped away from the platform and walked over to Mos.

Mos dropped to his knees and said, "God, I knew you would be here."

Steve looked down, "Mos, my emissary, no need to kneel. Stand."

Tutu walked over to Steve and stared intensely. The hood hid most of Steve's face and Tutu squirted. He strained to see detail but only saw shadowed outlines. "Tutu not believe in God. Hate Elder and you."

Steve grabbed Tutu, "Do not fight The Elder!" He gave Tutu a quick shock. "Ever!" He tossed him aside.

Tutu, terrified, shook. He blinked several times and remained on the ground.

Steve said, "I am here to guide you, but if you disobey and resist I can punish." He made a gesture for Erwin to amp up his volume for a few seconds on the hidden embedded speakers around the village. "Follow me and I reward. Disobey me or the Elder I will punish!" The threat reverberated throughout the village. The shelters vibrated, as designed, to echo Steve's words.

He walked over to Oscar. Lifted him up to his face and whispered, "Love Oscar. Follow. Treat later." Then said loudly, "Do not fight my Gemps! They are to be loved and cared for." He tossed Oscar aside. "Return home, Elder!"

Oscar, torn with feelings, ran off into the jungle. He made his way to his secret entry way. He heard Steve say 'Love Oscar. Follow. Treat later.' But was scared at what he saw. On some levels he comprehended what Steve was doing. On other levels he was still a chimp that feared the unknown. Technology was magic and powerful.

***

Grenier was half-way through his bowl of popcorn when the Colonel walked in. Grenier caught a whiff of whiskey seconds before the Colonel entered the observation room. It wasn't strong, but it was noticeable enough to know the Colonel liked his breakfast grains liquid.

Codper looked at Grenier and the bowl of

popcorn. He frowned at the man.

Grenier looked up and smiled. "Sorry, Colonel. You'll have to get your own bowl."

"No doubt," Codper said. He hardly contained the look of disgust.

"You missed the beginning, but it looks like this might be a good movie."

Codper stared at the screen. "I'm not liking this."

Grenier took a deep breath. "Okay, what is it you're not liking?"

"This whole farce."

"Colonel. Why are you here then?"

Codper wanted to deck Grenier.

"You knew from the beginning what this program was about. You knew what Steve would be doing. You watched this operation from day one and . . ."

"Hadn't thought it through. I didn't think this project would have gone this far."

"And now that you see it?" Grenier put the bowl of popcorn aside.

Codper didn't say anything.

"Colonel, this is going to be a problem." Grenier got up and walked out.

## Chapter 7

Codper made it to his room late. He had lunch, alone, in the cafeteria. Abominations! He thought. He canceled his meeting with the Duty Officers – there was nothing he wanted to talk about anyway. Captain Pierce had requested morning prayer sessions, but Codper hadn't committed. A conflict of interest lingered in the back of his mind. He sighed and scanned his desk. The bible was nearby, next to the keyboard. He walked over to his desk and sat. He reached over and grabbed the book, the comfort he needed. A random page:

*"And I said unto them, Whosoever hath any gold, let them break it off. So they gave it me: then I cast it into the fire, and there came out this calf.*

*And when Moses saw that the people were naked; (for Aaron had made them naked unto their shame among their enemies:)*

*Then Moses stood in the gate of the camp, and said, Who is on the Lord's side? let him come unto me. And all the sons of Levi gathered themselves together unto him." – Exodus 32:24-26*

His other comfort lay within a foot. It was a third full. His cup had dust in it. It always did when empty for more than an hour. He blew into it and wiped the lip clean. Some of the whiskey splashed droplets on his desk as he poured. Those he let dry. The one's that landed on his bible he wiped off. He randomly picked another page and read:

*"Draw out also the spear, and stop the way against them that persecute me: say unto my soul, I am thy salvation.*

*Let them be confounded and put to shame that seek after my soul: let them be turned back and brought to confusion that devise my hurt.*

*Let them be as chaff before the wind: and let the angel of the Lord chase them." – Psalm 35:3-5*

He said aloud, "God! Please give me a sign. I am torn over this. I want to do right but I need your guidance." He clicked on the email program on his computer and finished the cup. He poured another cup while a stream of subject lines scrolled down the screen. The stream stopped and one email caught his eyes. The title was, "New Assignment Orders. Read Immediately." That he opened. It was directly from the Joint Chief and it was brief. His official orders were on the way, but effective immediately he was fired. End of message. He nearly dropped his cup. After staring at the email for nearly five minutes he drained his cup, got up and walked out of his room.

***

Grenier was at his desk when he heard the new email indicator. It was from the Joint Chief. The first half of the email was what he expected. Codper was being replaced, immediately. The official orders were forthcoming. The second half of the email took him by surprise. He exclaimed, "Fuck!" The Colonel got his wish after all. "Bastard!" The ending confused him. He was to continue as Director of a new phase in the program. Steve, Kelly, and Oscar were to stay as consultants. His new orders would be sent in by carrier within the new few days. Odd. He got up and walked toward the door. This was something he had to talk to Steve about. Interesting he thought then he realized what the new phase would be. By the time he reached the door he was giddy. This was going to be a great day. As he started walking out he nearly bumped into Codper. Before he could say something Codper recoiled an arm and struck quickly. His fist connected with Grenier chin, launching him backwards into his desk. Grenier rubbed the hit off and braced himself for another attack.

Codper stepped past the room threshold. "You fuck! You had me replaced! I ought to kick your ass! You ruined my career!"

"You're the one who went Dark Age on me. You had one job to do and that came into question. What do you expect?"

"You blind-sided . . ."

"As if you hadn't tried to blind side me? The Chairman left you to hang, friend. You got eaten by your own kind."

"Non-sense!"

"You better fuck non-sense, because no one else will touch you."

Codper rushed in with an uppercut that felt air.

Grenier sidestepped and slammed an open palm into the Colonel's temple. He didn't want to kill the man, so he scaled the blow down.

Codper's head hit the edge of the desk. He collapsed and stayed down.

Grenier said, "You fuck! How dare you come into my office like this. You medieval son-of-a-bitch. Take your bible thumping ass and leave!"

Codper slowly got up. He realized Grenier had better skills. "This is not over," he hissed as he gave himself some distance from Grenier.

"The hell it better be over. Fuck with me and you could kiss your pension goodbye."

"Don't threaten me!"

"I just did. Now get the fuck out or I'll have you carried out breathing or otherwise. Your choice."

Codper eyed the younger man intensely. He had better skill that was certain. "This is not finished."

"Colonel, don't write checks with your mouth that your ass can't cash."

Codper backed out of the room, "Fuck you!"

"And that god damn stupid horse you rode in on." Grenier spat.

Seconds later all was quiet. Codper gone, Grenier sat in his chair. He'd give Steve and Kelly the news later. The silly pompous pious ass Grenier thought. One job and he couldn't do that right. He took several deep breaths to relax. After punching in the base intercom code on his phone he announced, "Attention all personnel. Attention all personnel. Colonel Codper has been relieved of duty by the Joint Chief of Staff. Under no circumstances are you obligated to follow his orders. His replacement is enroute. Until then, Captain Pierce is temporarily in charge." That should take care of most of the personnel he thought. It was the small faction of devotees that worried him. It was no secret the Colonel held bible studies on Sundays. It was also no secret that most of the attendees leaned just as far right if not further. Grenier sucked in his lips as he realized Captain Pierce leaned just as hard to the right. "Fuck!" was all he could say. He quickly tapped out a message to the Joint Chief.

*"Request immediate military personnel replacement. Predict conditions will devolve to dangerous levels."*

*Message sent.*

***

Captain Pierce knocked on the Colonel's door.

Codper had just finished nursing his fourth cup of whiskey when he heard the knock. He was not in the mood to have guests. He took another sip. "What?!?"

The Captain's voice from behind the door said, "Colonel, we need to talk."

"It's unlocked." Another sip.

Pierce walked in. "This is not right, sir."

Codper nodded and pursed his lips. "Yeah. Short of shooting the fuck I can't do anything."

Pierce eyed the older officer. He sucked air through his front teeth making a sharp smack sound. "Why don't you, sir?"

Codper looked up from his cup. "My pension. That's why I won't."

Pierce stepped in closer. "Sir, the little prick is playing with fire. Government project or not. It's not right. We know how you feel about those things. Most of us agree."

Codper stared the younger man in the eye. "It's your problem now."

Pierce nodded. "Not what I wanted to hear."

Codper drained his cup. The whiskey still stung on the way down. He hadn't drank enough to take care of that.

"Son, I've been doing this far too long. I'm tired. The world is fucked and you want me to kill my enemy?"

Pierce nodded, "Sounds about right."

Codper poured himself another. "What would you have me do? Take over the base. Murder everyone and blame those abominations?"

"It's still sounding right to me, sir."

Codper eyed the man.

"We could release the other Gemps, let them run wild in here. Afterward we burn this place to the ground. Grenade those with bullet wound to the head to remove traces."

"Thou shall not kill."

"Bullshit, Colonel! We are soldiers. That's what we do. These are our enemies. They are creating creatures outside of God's realm. You've been outspoken for weeks now. This is the time to do something."

Codper started to pour himself another drink when suddenly Pierce stopped him.

The young man held a vise grip on the bottle.

"Let go." Codper said.

"Sir, you in or out?"

"Let go."

Pierce released the bottle.

"I'm in. But we have to remove all traces."

Pierce smiled.   *** **End of Part 2** ***

## What is LightSail?

- LightSail is a citizen-funded mission to test solar sailing technology for CubeSats
- Solar sailing uses the sun's energy rather than chemical fuel to propel a spacecraft
- The Planetary Society has announced a test launch in early May 2015
- A second spacecraft will launch to a higher orbit to fully test solar sailing in 2016

LightSail is a citizen-funded project by The Planetary Society, the world's largest non-profit space advocacy group. The project aims to apply solar sailing, an innovative method of propulsion using the sun's energy, to CubeSats, which lack propulsion.

**About CubeSats:** CubeSats have made low-cost space missions a reality for universities and research groups. However, providing propulsion for these tiny satellites has been a major challenge that has limited their usefulness so far. LightSail will demonstrate the viability of solar sailing for CubeSats.

**LightSail's Test Flight:** The first LightSail spacecraft will embark on a test flight in May 2015, launched on an Atlas V rocket from Cape Canaveral Air Force Station in Florida. The mission will test LightSail's critical functions in low-Earth orbit, a precursor to a second mission slated for 2016.

The 2015 test flight will not carry the spacecraft high enough to escape Earth's atmospheric drag, and will thus not demonstrate controlled solar sailing. LightSail will test its attitude control system and study the behavior of the sails for a few days before it is pulled back into the planet's atmosphere.

**LightSail's Main Mission:** The 2016 mission will mark the first controlled, Earth-orbit solar sail flight and ride along with the first operational launch of SpaceX's Falcon Heavy rocket. LightSail will team up with Prox-1, a small spacecraft designed by the Georgia Tech to demonstrate automated rendezvous and inspection techniques.

**How Solar Sailing Works:** Light is made of packets of energy called photons. While photons have no mass, a photon traveling as a packet of light has energy and momentum. Solar sail spacecraft capture light momentum with large, lightweight mirrored surfaces—sails. As light reflects off a sail, most of its momentum is transferred, pushing on the sail.

The resulting acceleration is small, but continuous. Unlike chemical rockets that provide short bursts of thrust, solar sails thrust continuously and can reach higher speeds over time. Solar sailing is considered one possible means of interstellar space travel.

**LightSail's Hardware:** The Planetary Society's LightSail spacecraft is a three-unit CubeSat about the size of a loaf of bread, with Mylar sails measuring 32 square meters (344 square feet) packed inside. Each sail is just 4.5 microns thick—one-fourth the thickness of an average trash bag. Once in space, LightSail's solar arrays swing open, revealing the inside of the spacecraft and unwinding four tape measure-like metallic booms to unfold the four triangular sails.

Learn more at sail.planetary.org.

ONLI STUDIOS
RHYTHMISTIC GRAPHIC NOVELS
NOG NU!!
THE T-MONSTER COMETH!!
$5.00 USA With CD or Trading Cards.
ONLI, WOODS ST. PIERRE
NOG IS BACK!!
COLLECT ALL THREE BOOKS!
"THE WAR FOR PLANET NUBA"
IS COMING SOON FROM
THE RHYTHMISTIC STAFF OF
ONLI STUDIOS.
IN PRINT.  IN DOWNLOAD!
WWW. ONLISTUDIOS.COM
"FUN, FIRE & FUNK"
© TURTEL ONLI 2014  TM

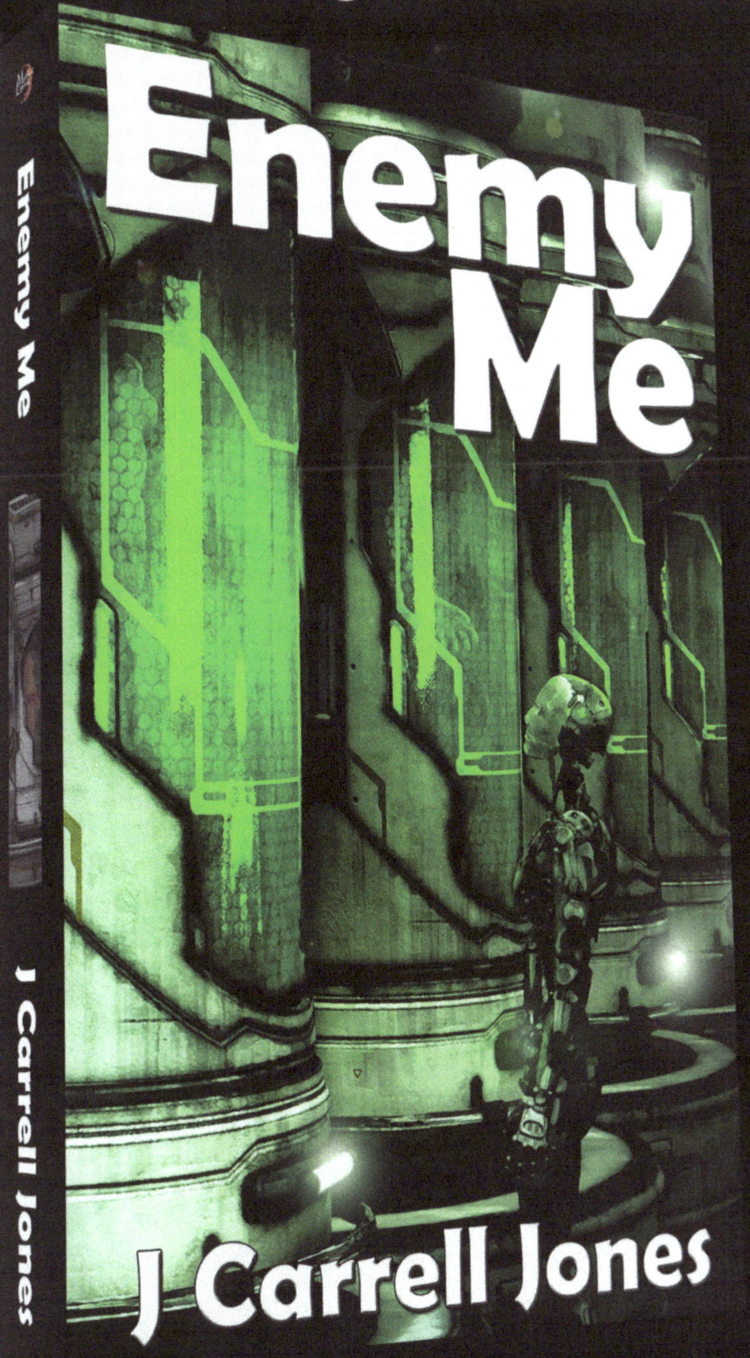

Pete Walker died . . . again . . .
and again . . .
and again . . . to save humankind.
Enemy Me
Enemy Me
J Carrell Jones
J Carrell Jones
Online or in print at Amazon.com

EXTRASOLAR

jrmalone.deviantart.com

bovistock.c

tart.com

The Luxury Cruiser Opulence
bovistock.deviantart.com
icfii 2012

Damefatale (cosplayer) reworked

J Carrell Jones

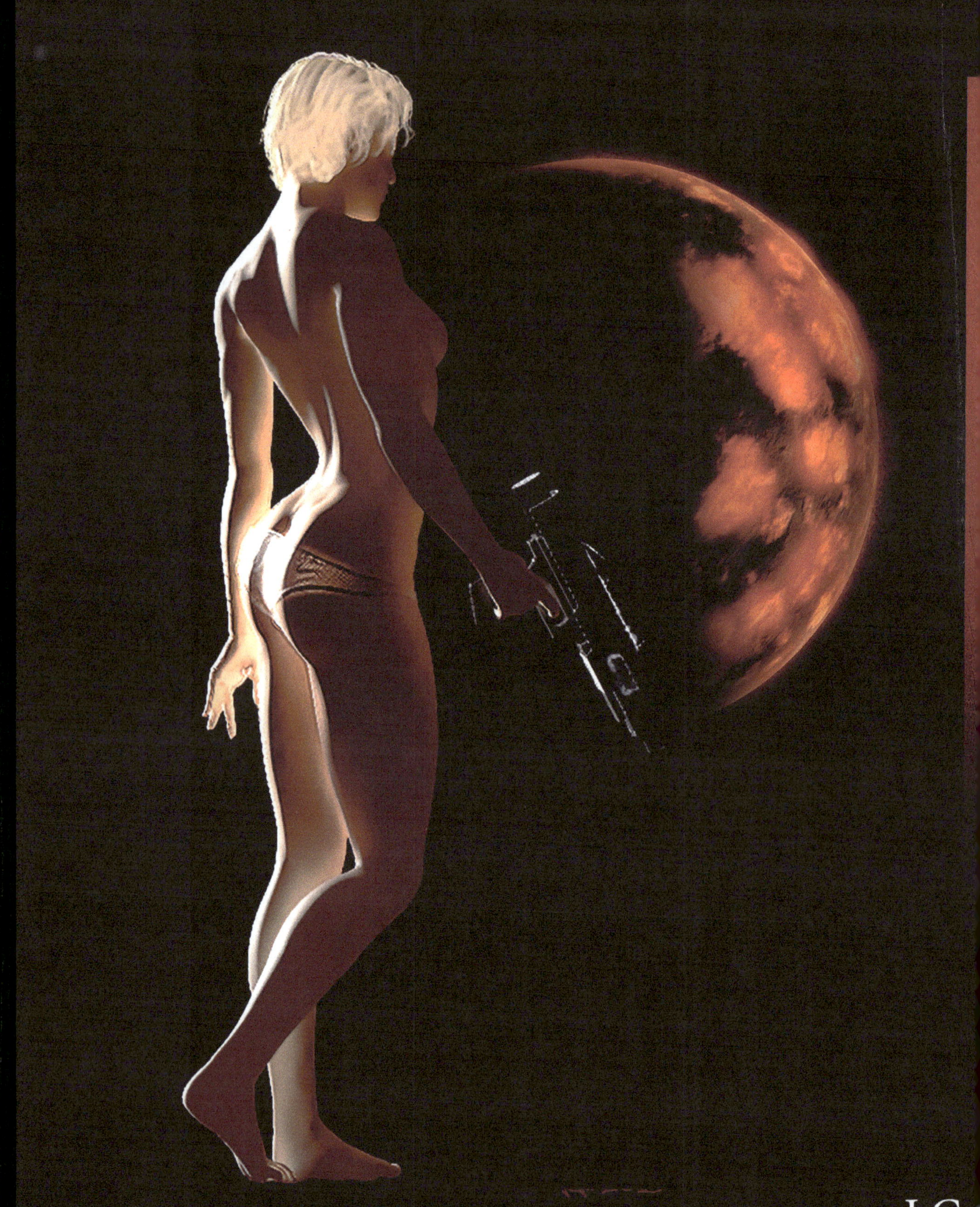
J Ca

ones

UNIVERSE BOUND
Imagination Engaged
Join the ranks of others who have allowed their minds to grab hold of the threads of tales. Hold fast, because the journey is about to start.
Welcome to the Universe Bound. Imagination engaged.
http:/mythicallegends.com

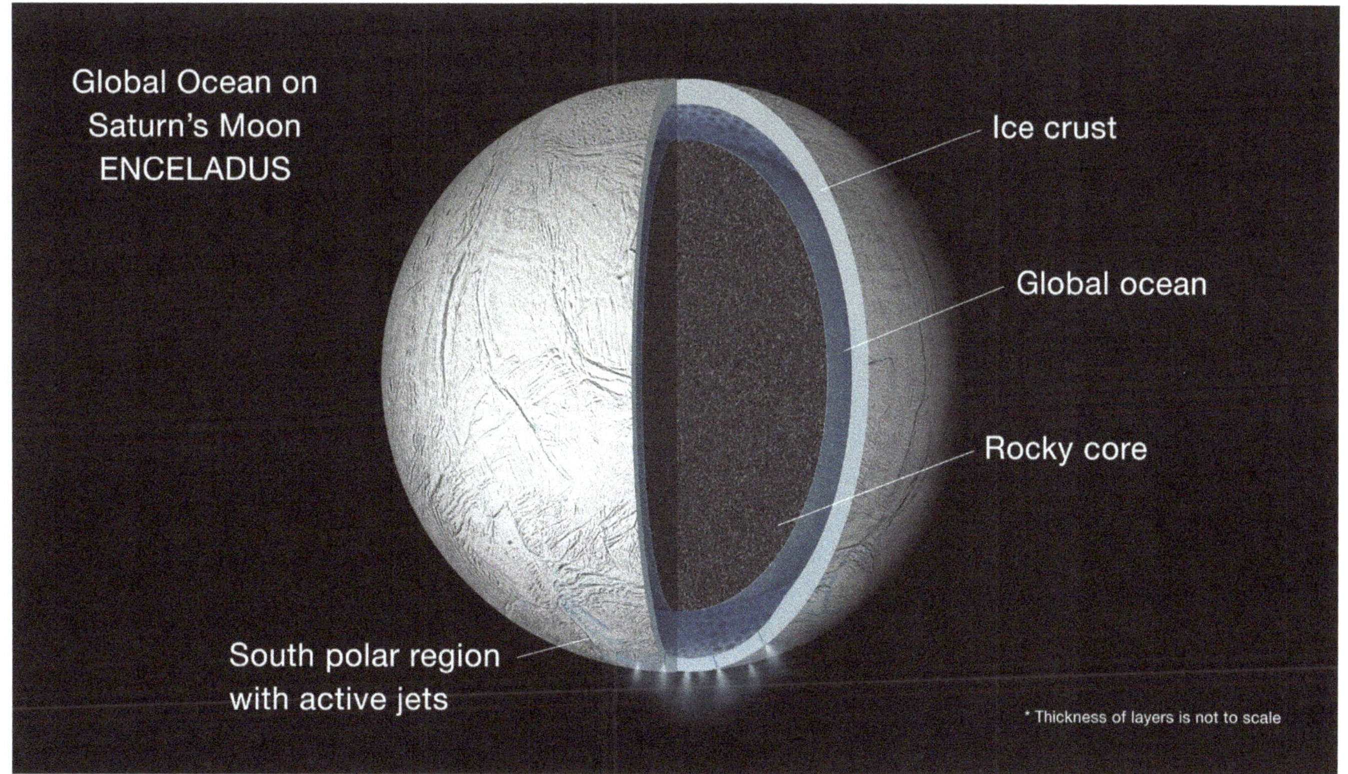


# Cassini Finds Global Ocean in Saturn's Moon Enceladus

**A global ocean** lies beneath the icy crust of Saturn's geologically active moon Enceladus, according to new research using data from NASA's Cassini mission.

Researchers found the magnitude of the moon's very slight wobble, as it orbits Saturn, can only be accounted for if its outer ice shell is not frozen solid to its interior, meaning a global ocean must be present.

The finding implies the fine spray of water vapor, icy particles and simple organic molecules Cassini has observed coming from fractures near the moon's south pole is being fed by this vast liquid water reservoir. The research is presented in a paper published online this week in the journal Icarus.

Previous analysis of Cassini data suggested the presence of a lens-shaped body of water, or sea, underlying the moon's south polar region. However, gravity data collected during the spacecraft's several close passes over the south polar region lent support to the possibility the sea might be global. The new results -- derived using an independent line of evidence based on Cassini's images -- confirm this to be the case.

"This was a hard problem that required years of observations, and calculations involving a diverse collection of disciplines, but we are confident we finally got it right," said Peter Thomas, a Cassini imaging team member at Cornell University, Ithaca, New York, and lead author of the paper.

Cassini scientists analyzed more than seven years' worth of images of Enceladus taken by the spacecraft, which has been orbiting Saturn since mid-2004. They carefully mapped the positions of features on Enceladus -- mostly craters -- across hundreds of images, in order to measure changes in the moon's rotation with extreme precision.

As a result, they found Enceladus has a tiny, but measurable wobble as it orbits Saturn. Because the icy moon is not perfectly spherical -- and because it goes slightly faster and slower during different portions of its orbit around Saturn -- the giant planet subtly rocks Enceladus back and forth as it rotates.

The team plugged their measurement of the wobble, called a libration, into different models for how Enceladus might be arranged on the inside, including ones in which the moon was frozen from surface to core.

"If the surface and core were rigidly connected, the core would provide so much dead weight the wobble would be far smaller than we observe it to be," said Matthew Tiscareno, a Cassini participating scientist at the SETI Institute, Mountain View, California, and a co-author of the paper. "This proves that there must be a global layer of liquid separating the surface from the core."

The mechanisms that might have prevented Enceladus' ocean from freezing remain a mystery. Thomas and colleagues suggest a few ideas for future study that might help resolve the question, including the surprising possibility that tidal forces due to Saturn's gravity could be generating much more heat within Enceladus than previously thought.

"This is a major step beyond what we understood about this moon before, and it demonstrates the kind of deep-dive discoveries we can make with long-lived orbiter missions to other planets," said co-author Carolyn Porco, Cassini imaging team lead at Space Science Institute, Boulder, Colorado, and visiting scholar at the University of California, Berkeley. "Cassini has been exemplary in this regard."

The unfolding story of Enceladus has been one of the great triumphs of Cassini's long mission at Saturn. Scientists first detected signs of the moon's icy plume in early 2005, and followed up with a series of discoveries about the material gushing from warm fractures near its south pole. They announced strong evidence for a regional sea in 2014, and more recently, in 2015, they shared results that suggest hydrothermal activity is taking place on the ocean floor.

Cassini is scheduled to make a close flyby of Enceladus on Oct. 28, in the mission's deepest-ever dive through the moon's active plume of icy material. The spacecraft will pass a mere 30 miles (49 kilometers) above the moon's surface.

The Cassini-Huygens mission is a cooperative project of NASA, ESA (European Space Agency) and the Italian Space Agency. NASA's Jet Propulsion Laboratory in Pasadena, California, manages the mission for the agency's Science Mission Directorate in Washington. JPL is a division of the California Institute of Technology in Pasadena. The Cassini imaging operations center is based at SSI. The California Institute of Technology in Pasadena manages JPL for NASA.

**For more information about Cassini, visit:**

http://www.nasa.gov/cassini

http://saturn.jpl.nasa.gov

Media Contact

Preston Dyches
Jet Propulsion Laboratory, Pasadena, Calif.
818-354-7013
preston.dyches@jpl.nasa.gov

Dwayne Brown / Laurie Cantillo
NASA Headquarters, Washington
202-358-1726 / 202-358-1077
dwayne.c.brown@nasa.gov / laura.l.cantillo@nasa.gov

2015-298

# MYTHICAL LEGENDS PUBLISHING

# WE CREATE DREAMS

http://mythicallegends.com

## Image Details

**Mission:** Mars Science Laboratory (MSL)

Target: **Mars**

Spacecraft: **Curiosity**

**Instrument:** Mars Hand Lens Imager (MAHLI)

**Views: 24,001**

# Looking Up at Mars Rover Curiosity in 'Buckskin' Selfie

**This low-angle** self-portrait of NASA's Curiosity Mars rover shows the vehicle at the site from which it reached down to drill into a rock target called 'Buckskin' on lower Mount Sharp.

COMIC REPUBLIC #1
GUARDIANPRIME
GENESIS
WE KNOW HIS MIGHT...
IT BEGAN HERE.
M'ART
IKECHUKWU
AWELENJE
COMIC REPUBLIC
NOV 2015
WWW.THECOMICREPUBLIC.COM

# Bibliography

## Kelly King

Kelly was born in Los Angeles, California, South LA Hoover Hospital many years ago. Kelly started writing at the age of 8. She loved reading fantasy stories and one day she decided to write one. She wrote the story in a small pink composition book given to her by her father. Her very first story was about a hamster who loved watermelon.

Kelly served in the Coast Guards' SAR (Search and Rescue). As a result, she has seen her share of fire fights, death, and dramatic rescues. The benchmark is Lives saved over Lives lost and Lives unaccounted for. Kelly currently lives in Bethesda, Maryland (she inherited her home from her Grandfather. Her parents were killed in a car accident when she was in her teens), with a Rabbit named Buck and a Cat named Rogers. Both own her and claim equal rights over her personage.

## Patricia I Williams

Born in New Orleans, La. and lived in Alexandria until she was twelve, Patricia I. Williams fell in love with Southern California on arrival. She would not want to live anywhere else, at least for this lifetime. She loves knowing the ocean is just beyond the hill and that Disneyland is the happiest place on earth. She enjoys traveling through the Southwest. The history and legends fuel a lot of imaginative Wild West adventures. She loves Science Fiction, film and books. Believes horses, dogs and cats are ideal companions.

## Kenneth A Strickland

Kenneth Strickland was born in 1958, a very good year because he showed up! He has a love for science fiction although he hasn't read everyone others say he should, he enjoys it greatly.

He is a grad of Westchester High School in Los Angeles, enjoys history, auto racing and animation. (No, he doesn't know the words to Let it Go...) Loves art, and loves taking the bus to the end of the line to see where it goes. He loves cooking, cars and music. He has studied comedy and film and animation and is working with a professional friend to produce a web series. He has worked in retail, and as a security guard (most boring!). Generally speaking, I like you when I meet you. Enjoys being a nerd. My first book was a joy to write, and I hope you enjoy it.

# Bibliography

### Brandon Hill

I am a native of Louisiana and current resident of Lafayette. An avid and frequent reader of science fiction and fantasy, I began writing in the eleventh grade. I am a graduate of McNeese State University in Lake Charles.

"I am a 'classic nerd' and hopeless romantic who loves sci-fi and fantasy, and am a prolific writer who has had dreams of authorship since childhood. I sketch perhaps even more prolifically than I write, and have drawings of just about every character my warped imagination has come up with. I hope to continue sharing these ideas, characters, and stories with others for years to come."

---

### Moshe Prigan

Moshe Prigan is a writer of short fiction and is currently writing a book. He lives in Haifa, Israel and he is a graduate of Haifa University in History and Political Sciences. His Hebrew stories have been published by Biglal Magazine and Stematsky's The Literary Greenhouse Anthology. His English fiction has been published in magazines as The Bear (Ireland), Tales from the Shadow Realm, Genesis Science Fiction, 34th Parallel, Witch Works, Fuck Fiction and A Quiet Courage. Another fiction is forthcoming in HOOT.

---

### J Carrell Jones

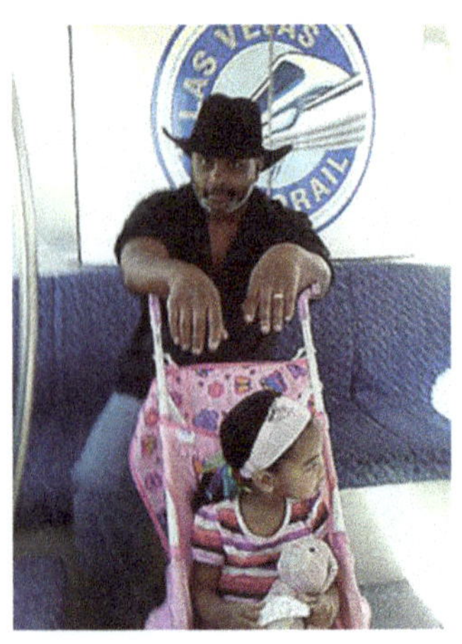

Born and raised in Southern California, J Carrell Jones, an Army Veteran, has worked in the Customer Support field for nearly 30 years. His interests are as vast as his imagination - 3D Content creating to writing to graphic design to voice overs. Currently, he lives in Inglewood, California with his wife, a beautiful daughter, a female cat named Perilous, a dozen fish, and two guinea pigs. The oldest is Hop and the younger one is named Guinea.

www.ingramcontent.com/pod-product-compliance
Lightning Source LLC
Chambersburg PA
CBHW042105160726
48295CB00017B/990